WITHDRAWN

"The fallout of an abandoned generati[...] parents and youth workers. Commo[...] understand. We all need the kind of [...] provides. I heartily recommend it to all who want to keep in touch with what many of today's youth are experiencing."

—PAUL FLEISCHMANN, president,
National Network of Youth Ministries

"This book is a bright light focused on the shadowy, dark phenomenon of self-injury. Using a solid foundation of biblical principles coupled with observations by professional therapists and personal experiences of those who have been there, Jerusha Clark and Dr. Earl Henslin bring a sense of hope to those who struggle with self-harm and a wealth of practical insights to those who seek to offer hope and healing."

—PHIL SWIHART, PhD, clinical psychologist;
director of counseling services, Focus on the Family

"If you are looking for help or trying to understand a cutter, you have found your resource. This book lives up to its title and makes sense of what goes on *Inside a Cutter's Mind*. Not only will you better understand the behavior but you will also find comfort, encouragement, direction, and most of all hope in this horrific trauma. Even in the midst of the pain, Jerusha and Dr. Henslin help us see the caring touch of the Creator."

—DAVE CARDER, coauthor of *Secrets of Your Family Tree*
and *Torn Asunder: Recovering from Extramarital Affairs*

"Literature on self-injury is incredibly relevant. *Inside a Cutter's Mind* provides both those who suffer from the illness and those loved ones close to them the opportunity to feel less alone and more informed on a growing epidemic."

—PLUMB, Curb recording artist

JERUSHA CLARK WITH DR. EARL HENSLIN

INSIDE A CUTTER'S MIND

UNDERSTANDING AND HELPING THOSE WHO SELF-INJURE

TH1NK
P.O. Box 35001
Colorado Springs, Colorado 80935

TH1NK is an imprint of NavPress.
TH1NK and the TH1NK logo are registered trademarks of NavPress. Absence of * in connection with marks
of NavPress or other parties does not indicate an absence of registration of those marks.

ISBN-10: 1-60006-054-4
ISBN-13: 978-1-60006-054-0

Cover design by Charles Brock | The Designworks Group; www.thedesignworksgroup.com
Cover photo by Shutterstock
Creative Team: Nicci Hubert, Kathy Mosier, Arvid Wallen, Kathy Guist

Clark, Jerusha.
  Inside a cutter's mind : understanding and helping those who
self-injure / Jerusha Clark with Dr. Earl Henslin.
     p. cm.
  Includes bibliographical references.
  ISBN 1-60006-054-4
  1. Self-mutilation. 2. Self-injurious behavior. 3. Psychotherapy.
I. Henslin, Earl R. II. Title.
  RC569.5.S45I5744 2007
  616.85'82--dc22

                          2006031775

Printed in the United States of America

1 2 3 4 5 6 7 8 9 10 / 11 10 09 08 07

To Jeramy Alan,
my beloved husband
and best friend.
It'll always be
you and me, against
the world.

CONTENTS

FOREWORD

To the average person it just doesn't make sense. Why would anyone deliberately hurt himself or herself? Isn't that crazy? Doesn't that go against human nature? Doesn't that go against the belief that we are self-protective organisms?

In this insightful and beautifully written book, *Inside a Cutter's Mind*, Jerusha Clark and Dr. Earl Henslin have done an excellent job explaining the self-harm phenomena in accessible language with vividly clear examples. More importantly, they have given sufferers and families a road map to healing. By adding the spiritual dimension to understanding and treating self-injurers, the authors, for the first time that I am aware of in books addressing this issue, provide practitioners and patients with a more comprehensive toolbox to overcome this potentially devastating problem.

I have treated many self-harmers over the years. This book rings true with my own clinical experience in many ways. Here's an example of how complex this problem can be: A twenty-three-year-old woman came to me for help with bulimia and depression. Through a combination of medication and psychotherapy, she showed significant improvement. After two years she ended treatment in a much healthier state than when she started. Eight years later, after a very stressful period at work, she started cutting on herself, at first lightly and then much more intensely. Initially she appeared to be having blackouts when the cutting occurred. She would have times she didn't remember. Through treatment we discovered that she had been sexually molested by a neighbor when she was five years old. As this book points out, prior abuse is common in cutters. I worked with her using various forms of treatment including EMDR, also discussed in this book, to deal with her past traumas. These techniques were very helpful for her. Additionally, I prescribed Naltrexone for her on the premise that cutting raises levels of endorphins, morphinelike substances that bring pleasure to the brain and thereby contribute to the addictive, repetitive behavior of cutting. Naltrexone blocks the effects of endorphins, so rather than causing relief from emotional pain, the cutting causes acute pain, as it would for any of us. Over time, this patient was able to stop her self-destructive behavior.

This case highlights many of the important factors with self-injurious behavior. It is often associated with other challenges, such as eating and mood disorders. Environmental factors, such as past abuse, often play an important role. Treatment usually involves biological and psychological therapies, both of which are discussed at length over the course of this book.

Cutting is not understood by the general public and the vast majority of mental-health professionals. This book is an important resource for us all.

Daniel G. Amen, MD,
author of *Change Your Brain, Change Your Life*

ACKNOWLEDGMENTS

I would like to acknowledge the following people:

Those who have courageously gone before me in writing about self-injury, especially Marilee Strong, Dr. Tracy Alderman, Steven Levenkron, V. J. Turner, Dr. Wendy Lader, Karen Conterio, and Caroline Kettlewell. The research you have done and the stories you share powerfully influenced my own writing. I am deeply indebted to each of you.

Kathy Hansen for modeling determined hope and allowing me to be up, down, or inside out depending on how well the book was going. Thank you, my cherished friend, for your help with the kids and your support of God's work in my life.

Kathy Moratto, whose wisdom and wit enrich my life immeasurably. I'm grateful God chose to bless me with your close friendship.

Kimberlie Farrow for taking care of Jocelyn and Jasmine with love, patience, and joy.

Lorraine Pintus, who lives what she writes and loves zealously. Thank you for continuing to mentor me.

Nicci Hubert for wanting (as much as I did) this book to be all that it could. You shaped my words with beauty, grace, and truth.

Christine Hammill, who is brave and fierce and altogether wonderful.

Marty and the entire staff at McDonald's #10979 for sharing your smiles (and electrical outlets) with me.

Marissa Lee, who graciously allowed me to pick her brain and mine her experience.

Gina Hoyt for lovingly befriending crazy, question-asking, never-satisfied-with-small-talk me.

Marsha Williams, who speaks truth and wisdom into my life and marriage.

Uncle Tom and Aunt Penny for your ever-loving, ever-loyal friendship and support.

Louie and Louise Moesta, who were ever on the lookout for new articles and who cared enough to both instruct me on the "proper" use of commas in a series and make sure that I stayed healthy and balanced during the intensive writing process.

Cameron Germann for being a trusted confidant and faithful friend.

My prayer team, who went in for round two and waged war on my behalf.

Kathy Mosier for being the kind of editor one looks forward to working with.

Spencer and Rona Clark, who have always loved me like their own.

J. A. C. and LeAnn Redford for your courage to live and parent with gracious vulnerability and persevering love.

Yahweh, my loving and just God, my strength in weakness and my refuge in times of trouble. You released me from the cords of death and have set me on the Rock higher than I. I praise and thank You.

INTRODUCTION

I'VE GOT TO DO SOMETHING

It all started during my sophomore year in high school. When I came home from a late soccer practice, I noticed my third-quarter progress report on the kitchen counter. Obviously someone had gotten to the mail before I could.

Not that I was totally ashamed of my grades. I had three As, for crying out loud. Two Bs. And one B minus.

But as I stood looking at the tiny printed letters, I heard Dad's voice echoing in every corner of my mind: "Jordan, how close is a B minus to a C? Do you actually expect to get a scholarship with a C on your report card? You know your mom and I can't afford to pay for college. This is your sophomore year. Things matter now. I just want you to care about your future as much as I do."

It wouldn't matter to him that I'd pulled my grade in Algebra II from the straight C I had at first semester's end to the B minus that glared back at me now. And I knew he wouldn't get "angry." He would just give me that cold, disappointed lecture and then sigh so heavily I'd swear my mom could hear it in the next room, where she would sit listening with hands folded and brow knit.

Lost in my thoughts, I guess I didn't hear him come in

through the door that led to our garage. In a split second, I realized my dad hadn't been home yet. That meant Mom had opened the offensive report card, not him. But I didn't have time to hide the evidence of my failure.

Before I could open my mouth to explain that I would *definitely* have a B by the time second semester ended, he snatched the flimsy computerized form and peered at it intently.

He didn't say anything, didn't even look at me. He just walked out of the kitchen and slammed the door to his bedroom.

His silence undid me. I raced to my room but cautiously closed the door, careful not to let it shut too loudly. Even though Dad had just slammed his own door, there's no way I would risk sending him into a "disrespecting our home and the household rules will not be tolerated" tirade by hurling my door against its frame.

Everything inside me wanted to scream, to punch a wall, to throw something and hear it shatter, see it break. It was all too much. The shame I felt, the anger I could never express. It was like a volcano started to erupt in my mind. Raging thoughts assaulted me in every imaginable way: *You idiot! You'll never be good enough. Did you really think you could make him happy? You're nothing but a fat, worthless failure.*

My anger melted into an agonizing desire to cry. But no tears came. Instead, emptiness and numb resignation overtook me again. Not knowing what else to do, I walked over to my desk and started to clear away the tools I'd used for my science project. When I picked up the art knife, the craziest thought came into my head.

Don't ask me why, because to this day I haven't figured it out, but the only thing I wanted to do was cut myself. So I did.

And as soon as blood started to trickle from the small incision I'd made, I felt this incredible relief. Everything got quiet.

I felt alive again. My racing mind stilled as I watched the bright red liquid cleanse me, center me, make everything okay.

What did you feel when you read sixteen-year-old Jordan's story? Shock? Fear? Concern? Pity? Disgust?

Did you feel sorrow, knowing that your friend or child, your spouse or student may have had a similar first experience with self-injury? Did you feel paralyzed, unable to understand why someone would resort to such extremes? Did you empathize with Jordan? Have you felt the same stinging anguish of self-contempt and suppressed rage?

If someone you love intentionally hurts himself or herself, you may have run the gamut of these emotions—frustration, anxiety, despair, helplessness, confusion, desperation, and even repulsion. Maybe you've felt all of them at once.

Maybe, more than anything else, you have wanted to run away, to withdraw from the unnerving, painful reality. Still, the idea that your loved one might take a blade or a cigarette lighter to his or her own skin haunts you like a waking nightmare. Saying the wrong thing terrifies you. But you have to, you want to, do something. Maybe you feel embarrassed, ashamed, or alone.

YOU ARE NOT ALONE

I first confronted the issue of self-injury while working with high school students in Southern California. On a retreat with ten fourteen- to eighteen-year-olds, two of my coleaders discovered that seven of them had experimented with self-inflicted violence. The news shocked and frightened me.

Shortly thereafter, I helped host an evening discussion about self-harm. The stories that emerged, the pain that poured out, and the confusion that surrounded self-wounding impulses and behaviors compelled me to do something about the problem that obviously affected many in my life.

As I talked with more people, I learned that self-injury did not afflict only the teenage girls I knew. Peers of mine confessed battling self-harm, and the tales of self-wounding men, young and old, confronted me as well.

There was no way I could do it alone. So I enlisted the help of Dr. Earl Henslin, a psychologist whose twenty-plus years of work with hurting people have equipped him to guide others in understanding self-inflicted violence.

Dr. Henslin helped me wade through the psychotherapeutic and medical journals that likely would have daunted me had I attempted to tackle them on my own. He allowed me to enter into his vast wealth of experience with self-harm and the individuals who battle it. And he agreed to share some of it with you in his own writing. While the stories he has chosen to tell (details of which have been altered to protect individuals) will be separated into sections entitled *In My Experience*, I would like to acknowledge that Dr. Henslin's work on behalf of this book extends far beyond these segments.

For instance, Dr. Henslin introduced me to Dr. Daniel Amen, a colleague of his and a pioneer and forerunner in the field of neuropsychiatry. Dr. Amen graciously allowed me to interview him and gave Dr. Henslin and me access to his database of SPECT scans, a form of brain imaging that helps professionals and laypeople alike better understand the role of physiology in the struggles many of us face.

I want you to know from the outset: Self-inflicted violence is all at once a psychological, physical, and spiritual battle. Consequently, this book will examine all three aspects. But we will do so with balance and patience, recognizing that discussing biochemistry, psychoemotional issues, and spirituality can be intimidating.

THE STORY THAT INFORMS US

After Dr. Henslin and I had finished writing the majority of this book, I came across a heartbreaking account. The grief I felt hearing Janice's story compelled me to revise the introduction I had initially composed.

Janice is a young mother whose love, sensitivity, and desire to end an agonizing battle with self-injurious impulses recently prompted her to seek counsel from a therapist in her area.

Within the first few sessions, after she had begun to spill the contents of her wounded heart in this man's confidence, Janice listened as her therapist spoke these dreadful words: "I just want to let you know that I've never seen anyone fully recover from the urge to self-harm."

How can the Janices we know fight for recovery with counsel like this? Is there any hope for the Janices we love, want to help, and struggle to understand?

I decided to write *Inside a Cutter's Mind* because I believe that a vigorous and tangible hope can be found. I have witnessed the freedom of people brought back from the brink of self-destruction. In their lives, the power of redemption overcame the pull of devastation.

But I have not merely observed redemption at work. I have personally experienced the wholesale rescue of my mind, body, and soul from the ravages of self-annihilating compulsion. Redemption came to me in the person of Jesus Christ.

Undeniably and unashamedly, this book is informed and framed by my faith in a God whose business is the recycling grace that makes beauty of ashes and turns what might destroy us into what ultimately gives us strength and hope. And because self-inflicted violence threatens the whole person, our journey toward understanding will be spiritual, though not strictly so.

This book is simultaneously founded on the research of gifted, diligent scholars who devote their lives to understanding the physiological and psychological dimensions of the human condition.

Consequently, my hope is that whether or not you consider yourself a spiritual person, whether or not you believe that God has anything to do with overcoming self-injury, you would find within this book the help and hope you need to understand and love people who self-harm.

I wish you could have traveled with me through each new layer of information and emotion that marked my journey toward comprehending self-inflicted violence. But since you could not, I hope that in my synthesizing the amazing, heart-wrenching, and hopeful things I have learned, you will be able to arrive at the same place of expanded understanding for and capacity to love self-harmers.

You have made an important and commendable decision to explore this difficult topic. When it comes to self-injury, we need to be equipped, encouraged, and educated.

We all approach this subject with our own concerns, fears, and perceptions. Some will be worried that they cannot be what their friend or loved one needs. Others will wonder if they have the time and energy to invest in coming alongside a self-wounder: *I have my own life, my own worries. Can I really do this?* Still others have tried to help, but feel hopeless: *What if the person I love never gets better?*

Clearly, if you picked up this book, you care deeply for the self-harmer(s) you know. But will the effort it takes to read about this challenging issue, not to mention putting the things you learn into practice, be worth it?

Yes.

I'd like to ask you, as far as you are able, to press into the concerns that weigh on you, the fears that threaten to paralyze you, and the biases that may hold you back. If you are willing to read without knowing for sure if you "have what it takes" or if the one you love will ever heal, I believe that you will find hope and help.

When you're ready, let's embrace the process together.

THEN AND NOW
A SURVEY OF SELF-INJURY

Diana Spencer seemed to be living every little girl's dream. After working as a nanny, a waitress, and even a cleaning woman, Di (as friends called her) began dating an older man. And not just any man, but the heir to Britain's throne—the Prince of Wales.

Almost the moment Prince Charles began pursuing Diana, the press—and most of the world—was captivated by this charming, strikingly beautiful young woman.

At only twenty years of age, after a rather short courtship and engagement, Diana Spencer married Prince Charles in St. Paul's Cathedral. The wedding was broadcast in seventy-four countries and watched by 750 million people worldwide. Diana was the first nonroyal English woman to marry an heir to the throne in over three hundred years.

During the ceremony the archbishop of Canterbury remarked, here is "the stuff of which fairy tales are made."[1] Around the globe, wistful women and girls sighed in agreement.

But this fairy tale was strictly an illusion. When Diana discovered that Prince Charles loved a former girlfriend more than he loved her, I can only imagine the grief and betrayal she felt.

Princess Di bore her first son less than a year into her ill-fated marriage. At twenty-one, I wonder if Diana felt trapped by endless royal duties, a cold and distant husband, and her new role as a mother.

Still, during her twelve-year marriage to Prince Charles, Diana worked tirelessly on behalf of charities around the world. She became "a symbol of selfless humanity, a standard-bearer for the rights of the truly downtrodden."[2] Her physical beauty deepened and matured. Many viewed Princess Di as the very essence of style and grace.

Diana also intentionally cut her skin, repetitively forced herself to vomit, and once deliberately threw herself down a flight of stairs.

When Princess Di first confessed her experiences with cutting, bulimia, and other forms of self-injury, the world sat up and took notice. Other pieces of the puzzle fell into place when journalist Andrew Morton published his biography *Diana: Her True Story.* Controversy surrounded the book even before it hit the shelves. But though no one knew it until after her death, Princess Diana collaborated with Morton on the work.

In it, Di revealed that Charles treated her struggles as melodramatic attempts to get attention. He wanted her to quit "faking it." Apparently, even Di's hurling herself down the staircase wasn't enough to faze the prince. He simply ignored Diana and went riding.

Princess Di's story reminds us that self-injury can afflict people in any walk of life. In fact, as many as eight million men and women deliberately harm themselves.[3] If we counted every loved one affected by another's self-injury, the number would likely be double or triple that figure.

Still, most of us know very little about self-harm. Steven Levenkron, one of the first psychotherapists to treat self-injurers, aptly noted, "Aside from the current publicity, most of which is sensational, unhealthily explicit, and serves only to frighten and disgust people, we are still largely in the dark about the phenomenon of self-mutilation."[4]

In order to truly understand and help those who self-wound, we will work to dismantle what the sensationalized media tells us about self-inflicted violence. We will also endeavor to debunk myths many of us have heard, believed, and even propagated. To do this, we'll need to learn both general and specific truths about self-harm.

So let's begin by looking at what modern-day self-injury looks like, the scope of this phenomenon, and historical and cultural factors that have played a role in the spread of self-inflicted violence.

WHAT IS SELF-INJURY?

The act of intentionally wounding oneself goes by many names. Self-injury, self-harm, self-inflicted violence, and self-mutilation are the most commonly employed terms. Vernacular descriptions such as cutting, burning, slashing, or scorching reveal specific methods people use to wound themselves. Medical professionals use other descriptors, including Deliberate Self-Harm Syndrome[5] and Self-Injurious Behavior Syndrome (SIBS).[6]

Dr. Armando Favazza, a pioneer in the research and treatment of self-injury, describes the phenomenon as "a morbid form of self-help."[7] And therapists Karen Conterio and Dr. Wendy Lader, founders of the first inpatient treatment center for self-harmers, use vivid expressions such as the "wounding embrace."[8]

We understand self-injury best when we synthesize all these terms. Self-harm is an act of violence inflicted by and against the self. Self-injurers use a wounding, morbid method to help, even nurture, themselves. And for some people, self-inflicted violence can become a serious medical condition, much like other emotional/physical syndromes.

I try to refrain from using the term *self-mutilation*, though you will notice that some of the academic and medical resources I quote from use this expression. Because most self-injurers recoil from this term and many self-wounders never *intend* to mutilate their bodies, I find *self-harm* and *self-injury* more appropriate phrases.

The majority of sufferers, like Jordan, whom we met in the introduction, or Princess Diana, cut or burn because they seek relief from seemingly uncontrollable pain or deadening numbness. Scars and physical damage are certainly results of self-injury, but mutilation is usually not the primary aim. Only when referring to advanced cases of self-harm will I use terminology such as *syndrome* or *addiction*.

Likewise, as you care for and work with people who self-injure, I urge you to choose your words carefully. When in doubt, listen to the language the person who self-harms uses and mirror his or her vocabulary. This both honors individuals and their unique experiences and shows a desire to meet them on their turf.

THE SELF-INJURER'S WORLD

Self-inflicted violence has many forms, but these are the most common:

- Cutting
- Burning
- Interfering with the healing of wounds
- Hitting, bruising
- Biting (including injurious nail biting)
- Harmful scratching or picking of the skin
- Pulling or plucking hair to an excessive degree
- Intentionally breaking one's bones
- Purposefully avoiding medical care for serious injuries

People who self-harm may inflict only superficial damage on their skin. Their wounds may require simple cleansing and time to heal. Other injuries break the skin, causing minor to moderate bleeding. And others require extensive medical repair, including stitches, bone-setting, or surgery. Permanent damage — scars, bald spots, or improperly healed bones — can result from extreme forms of self-injury.

Sufferers often experiment with various types of self-harm before finding a "preferred method." Cutting and burning are by far the most commonly encountered forms of self-injury, but hitting, biting, and scratching are also prevalent among self-harmers. Trichotillomania — the obsessive, repetitive pulling out of one's own hair for the relief of tension — is the only form of self-inflicted violence currently listed in the Diagnostic and Statistical Manual of Mental Disorders, fourth edition. The intentional breaking of one's bones, the amputation of limbs, and enucleation (eye gouging) are less commonly used (and obviously more extreme) methods of self-injury.

Fortunately, identified occurrences of the most radical forms of self-wounding are rare. But just how common are the more prevalent types of self-wounding—cutting, burning, and bruising? How big a problem are we talking about?

WE'RE JUST BEGINNING TO FIGURE IT OUT

Thirty to forty years ago, therapists and doctors helped "demystify" anorexia nervosa and bulimia, as well as develop treatment options for other forms of eating disorders. We are in the midst of a similar process with self-injury. Counselors and psychiatrists, social workers and college professors, parents and pastors are working together to understand and create viable recovery options for those who deliberately harm themselves.

I feel honored to be part of this important but difficult movement toward understanding. By reading this book, you are joining others who want to know about and come alongside self-injurers.

Many of us—I'd venture to guess most of us—have been personally affected by self-harm, whether in our home, school, workplace, or church. But formulating precise statistics about self-injury presents a nearly insurmountable problem.

The shameful, secretive nature of self-inflicted violence; the elaborate excuses, justifications, and even denial of people who harm themselves; and the inability to determine whether some deaths are the unintended result of cutting or intentional suicides make it particularly difficult to confirm exactly what percentage of the population currently self-injures.

What we do know is that the numbers are rising. A 2004 British report documented a 65 percent increase over two years in the number of hotline callers who struggled with self-harm.[9] In the United States, references to and articles about self-injury in the popular media rose from none in 1984 to 210 in 2004.[10] According to the *Los Angeles Daily News*, the L.A. Unified School District's suicide prevention hotline fielded six hundred calls about self-inflicted violence in a single eighteen-month period.[11] The most frightening aspect of that statistic is that it reflects only one hotline in one school district in one major city.

Cornell University has launched a focused research program on self-injurious behavior in adolescents and young adults, the National Institute of Mental Health maintains that self-inflicted violence ranks in the top ten mental conditions for women,[12] and a variety of private treatment centers serving both male and female self-harmers have sprung up around the country and abroad.

Dr. Michael Hollander directs one of these centers, the Two Brattle Center in Cambridge, Massachusetts. Hollander, a trained psychologist, relates, "Every clinician says it's increasing. . . . I've been practicing for 30 years, and I think it's gone up dramatically."[13] Other professionals—including many psychotherapists, clergy, and social workers—agree with Hollander.

The escalating incidence of self-injury recently prompted educators and activists to join those involved in the mental-health-care community to declare March 1 "Self-Injury Awareness Day."

Academics and clinicians argue about the reasons behind this evident swell in self-wounding behavior. Some believe a greater awareness of the problem and the willingness of more people to discuss this previously taboo subject simply brought to light what has always been happening. Others maintain that people are actually engaging in more self-injurious acts than ever before. And some claim that pop culture's sensationalized reporting on the issue has created this outbreak of self-inflicted violence. Still others assert that clinicians and laypeople—particularly those who previously viewed self-injury exclusively as a symptom of other psychological disturbances—have become better able to identify self-harm as an issue unto itself.

Perhaps the answer can be found in a combination of these factors, as well as in discerning how historical and cultural factors have influenced and continue to shape the phenomenon of self-injury.

MODERN CULTURE AND SELF-HARM

Princess Diana may have been one of the first celebrities to confess her battle with self-inflicted violence, but there certainly have been more. A-list actors and actresses have come forward, recounting their tales of agonized self-wounding. Famous recording artists — from hard-core rockers to easygoing folk singers — have shared their stories through lyrics and interviews.

Journalist Jeffrey Kluger sees this trend as simultaneously encouraging and devastating. He writes,

> Though it's true that such public disclosures encourage ordinary kids to come forward, it's also true that when glamorous people suffer from something, a bit of the glitter rubs off on the condition. . . . Then there is the Internet, where cutting chat rooms are just a keystroke away. Many offer support for kids who want to stop, but just as many wink at the problem and even subtly [in the worst cases unabashedly] encourage it.[14]

On blogspot.com, 1,547 posts matched a search for cutting and self-injury. Typing the words *cutting, self,* and *blood* into xanga.com's search engine yielded 15,878 links.

Scores of personal or group websites feature photos of and quotes from famous self-harmers. Chilling online journals often include graphic details about when, where, and why people hurt themselves. The most brazen (and perhaps the most brokenhearted?) bloggers include pictures of their wounds along with gory descriptions of techniques used to inflict them.

While researching self-injury for a screenplay, my dear friend Kelly observed,

> A lot of cutters are part of blogrings where they chronicle their experiences. In the process, they develop an online community/ family that actually winds up supporting and perpetuating their disorder, because if they stop cutting, they no longer belong. Most of them talk about "trying to get well," but there is still the underlying notion that getting well means getting kicked out of your online clique.

Like many other blogringing self-injurers, one with the screen name Seldom Understand doesn't think he needs "outside help." He declares, "I don't need therapy; this [blogging] is my therapy."

There can be little doubt: Modern culture influences the phenomenon of self-injury. But it's almost impossible to identify exactly how much or how negatively. Pop culture certainly did not create the problem. Long before music, television, film, and the Internet existed, self-inflicted violence played a significant role in the human experience. It's time to add some historical perspective to the modern-day one we've begun to formulate.

SELF-INJURY THROUGH THE AGES[15]

One of the first published references to self-injury occurred in the fifth century BC. Book VI of Herodotus' *History* describes a Spartan leader who deliberately and severely mutilated himself with a knife.[16]

Around 300 BC the "Father of Western Medicine," Hippocrates, developed a theory that people could be "rebalanced" by bloodletting, blistering, vomiting, purgatives, or potions that would cleanse the body. Ancients tried to "purify" themselves in a number of these life-endangering ways. Descriptions of these behaviors recorded in early texts resemble the self-destructive behaviors that we might call cutting, burning, or purging. Indeed, many modern self-injurers report a similarly strong urge to "cleanse" themselves from inner disease, perceived or actual (more on this later).

And surprisingly, biblical references to self-injurious behaviors outnumber those in any other historical source. Three times in the books of Leviticus and Deuteronomy alone, Jehovah commands the people of Israel not to cut their bodies ritually, as the pagan nations around them do (see Leviticus 19:28; 21:5; Deuteronomy 14:1-2).

One can learn of dramatic acts of self-inflicted violence by reading the epic duel on Mount Carmel. While Elijah and the Israelites watched, the frenzied priests of Baal "prayed louder and louder, cutting themselves with swords and knives—a ritual common to them—until they were covered with blood" (1 Kings 18:28, MSG). The worshipers of Baal believed their god could be pleased and provoked to action by their own blood sacrifice. In an effort to demonstrate whole-body commitment and surrender, Baal's priests sliced themselves unmercifully. They cut because they wanted their god to notice and *do* something.

The New Testament gospel of Mark chronicles the tragic and isolated existence of a man who deliberately, repeatedly slashed himself with stones (see 5:1-20). And after the death and resurrection of Christ, men and women in search of piety practiced self-injury in what they viewed as an expression of faith. Cults of flagellants starved, purged, scarred, whipped, and scourged themselves. Some even impaled their breasts, amputated limbs, gouged their eyes from the protective sockets in their skulls, or castrated themselves.

Flagellants wrote and spoke about their longing to imitate the sufferings of Jesus, as well as to mitigate divine judgment, which they often thought close at hand. During the Great Plague, flagellation increased among people who wished to atone for the sins they believed had brought the Black Death upon the world.

But self-inflicted violence of this kind is not unique to Christianity. Certain adherents of nearly every world religion—including Islam, Hinduism, and Buddhism—have translated religious devotion into self-destructive activities. Each behavior serves a specific purpose for the faith of both individual and community.

In Morocco, a group of mystical Islamic healers have long practiced self-injurious ceremonies. These dervishes work themselves into a ritual frenzy (a remarkable display of spinning dizziness, from which we derive the term *whirling dervish*) and lacerate their own heads. The injured and ill dip bits of bread and sugar cubes into the spilled blood, eat them, and reputedly receive healing in the process. For these people, blood is the most potent medicine.

Some Hindus use body modification to gain favor with their god Murugan. Ancient Aztecs and Maya displayed penitence by spilling their blood on sacred items. And Buddhists esteem self-denial, which sometimes becomes injurious, as a way to attain ecstatic degrees of holiness.

In a less dramatic fashion, children often use blood to bond with each other. Making small cuts on their fingers or using wounds that have been previously opened, they become blood brothers or sisters.

When people use the expression "getting rid of bad blood," they touch upon a deeply felt, if seldom directly expressed, symbol. Pure blood represents a healing agent not just for the body (for example, the earliest doctors "letting blood" from ailing patients) but also for the psyche. When people feel at peace with one another, we might say there's no "bad blood" between them.

In virtually every culture and every age, blood signifies the very essence of life. Blood spills out when new life is brought forth in childbirth and drains from an extinguished life in death. As Leviticus 17:11 proclaims, "The life of the body is in the blood" (NCV). And as we know, life involves more than a functioning body; God makes possible every aspect of life—its incomparably rich mysteries, the heights of joy, and the depths of sorrow—through the blood that sustains us.

It's fascinating to me that from the beginning of time and across the entire world, people have inherently sensed the truth that "blood, representing life . . . brings . . . atonement" (Leviticus 17:11). And in mystical and powerful ways, humans have always responded to the reality that blood shed in the right way can lead to peace, to *life*.

In his classic tale of good and evil *The Lion, the Witch and the Wardrobe*, C. S. Lewis describes this innately felt truth as "Deep Magic from the Dawn of Time." Even the most depraved character in Lewis's novel, the White Witch, Jadis, acknowledges and respects this law.

Coming to Edmund, her prisoner (who betrayed his brother and sisters out of vanity and greed), Jadis declares, "You know that every traitor belongs to me as my lawful prey and that for every treachery I have a right to a kill." She continues, "Unless I have blood as the Law says, all Narnia will be overturned and perish in fire and water."[17]

The rightful King, Aslan, strikes a bargain with the Witch, offering to exchange his innocent blood for Edmund's. Jadis gleefully accepts, happy to take the life of the powerful, royal lion in exchange for a mere human. Later, she taunts Aslan while bringing the knife upon him: "Fool . . . you have lost your own life and you have not saved his. In that knowledge, despair and die."[18]

But Lewis continues,

> Though the Witch knew the Deep Magic, there is a Magic deeper still which she did not know. Her knowledge goes back only to the dawn of time. But if she could have looked a little further back, into the stillness and the darkness before Time dawned, she would have . . . known that when a willing victim who had committed no treachery was killed in a traitor's stead . . . Death itself would start working backwards.[19]

Though it may be very difficult to grasp right now, self-injurers sometimes wound themselves because they innately, subconsciously know that in this world, as in Narnia, "The law says that almost everything must be made clean by blood, and sins cannot be forgiven without blood to show death" (Hebrews 9:22, NCV).

Across the ages, people of every age and station have inflicted violence on themselves in a desperate effort to make things right, to atone for their wrongs, to turn the tide of suffering backward.

In Narnia, only the noble and pure blood of the King could save Edmund. Likewise, in our nonfictional, spiritual world, *only* the once-for-all spilling of perfectly innocent blood, the blood of the Rightful Ruler of this world, can make a wrong world right and finally triumph over death. Many of us instinctively know this, but those who wound themselves have believed a twisted, toxic version of this beautiful, if bloody, truth.

Men and women of all kinds have bought into the lie that they can do something to turn back the tide of deadly pain. Harming the self to stave off the flow of emotional anguish, to feel something rather than stay numb forever, or to "pay" for mistakes is a bodily, mentally, and spiritually excruciating way to deal with life. And this is why healing from self-injury must be—all at once—physical, emotional, *and* spiritual.

In some ways, considering the historical evidence, self-inflicted violence is merely one of many "universal [if maladaptive] defense mechanisms to which people have always resorted in order to avoid a sense of dread—whether in terms of believing themselves literally damned or feeling emotionally tormented."[20]

Still, reading about the methods of and history behind self-harm may unnerve you. It did me. I found it particularly confusing that people would use pain to comfort themselves. It seemed paradoxical to me that wounding the self by drawing blood or breaking a bone could relieve deep emotional and spiritual distress. But this is exactly what self-harmers do and experience.

We've all watched movies or television shows in which a frantic, out-of-control person is "slapped" back to reality by a well-intentioned friend or colleague. The stinging pain of a slap ends the person's hysteria, and he or she often turns to thank the very person who inflicted the wound with the words, "I really needed that."[21]

For many, self-harm acts as the "slap" that distracts them from the overwhelming circumstances and ferocious thoughts and emotions that threaten to spin them completely out of control. The self-injurer acts the roles of both the frantic protagonist and the well-meaning, if temporarily harmful, friend.

So is it possible for outsiders—people who have never intentionally wounded themselves—to not only understand but empathize with the impulses behind self-injury?

From all I have learned, the answer is yes. Absolutely. Undeniably.

2 WHAT WORDS CANNOT EXPLAIN
WHY AND HOW SELF-INJURY BEGINS

While researching and writing this book, I encountered all kinds of people, each with his or her own ideas and assumptions about self-injury. And, sadly, most of the men and women I spoke with seemed eager to dismiss self-wounding with simplistic explanations.

On one particularly memorable occasion, a man approached me at Starbucks, curious about the pen scanner I use to upload significant information from books or articles I read. When he found out that I was writing about self-inflicted violence, he chuckled.

"Oh, that," he said. "Those people just want attention, you know."

"Actually . . ." I started to say.

But I quickly saw that this man had no interest in learning more about the phenomenon of self-harm or the people who suffer through it. He went on about other "attention-getting things" that "kids these days resort to" until the barista called his name and set the soy latte he'd ordered on the bar.

One morning at church, I chatted with a family I've known for several years. They are genuinely loving people, faithful and authentic. After asking about my work on this book, they intently listened to my response. So when one of them asked, "Don't you find that it all starts with a low self-esteem?" I expected they would hear me out in the same attentive manner.

Unfortunately, this family seemed content to simplify self-harm with a concise (but rather nebulous) explanation. Though I attempted to convey some of the complexities of how and why people begin self-injuring, they cut me off mid-sentence: ". . . which all goes back to low self-esteem."

I suspect that most of you know (at least intellectually) that simple explanations like these don't clarify, let alone reconcile, the painful reality of self-inflicted violence. But I also know that many of us just want something we can hold on to: an answer for the "why" and specific direction on how we can help.

For those of us stuck between what we know and what we long for, here is the news, both good and bad: There are no formulas for healing, especially the deep, whole-body healing that self-wounding necessitates. There are, however, some important clues for understanding why people start self-injuring and how we can help them stop. We can find these clues by investigating how people first begin and then continue to hurt themselves. Let's turn our attention to these matters now.

IN THE BEGINNING

If self-inflicted violence begins with very human, common feelings of sadness, anger, loss of control, and rejection, why doesn't everyone do it? Aside from the obvious answer that most of us are afraid of and actively avoid pain, there are other explanations for why some people start self-injuring while others don't.

I have to confess that before I knew better, I assumed that teenage girls started self-harming because they heard about it on TV or from someone else who did it. In reality, while media and social contagion often play roles in a person's experimentation with self-inflicted violence, these are not the most common motivations for people who begin a pattern of self-injury. Actually, the initial impetus for self-harm most often reported startled me. Again and again, in psychiatric and academic journals, in books and on the Internet, I read accounts of people who reported that the idea "just came to them." And my interviews with self-wounders confirmed this trend.

In *The Scarred Soul*, psychotherapist Tracy Alderman explains, "Most people who engage in self-inflicted violence have little or no idea of how they actually began to do so. An overwhelming number of individuals can cite no definitive event. They cannot remember how they learned of SIV, and they state that their self-injurious behaviors 'just happened.'"[1]

Over and over, self-harmers chronicled feeling anger, anxiety, or sorrow so deep that it seemed the world was unraveling around them. In the midst of this chaos, a thought "popped" into their mind: *You can cut* [or burn or break] *this out of you*. Or, even more insidiously, *You* must *cut* [or burn or break] *yourself until the pain goes away*.

One self-injurer, Mandy, describes the desire to cut as being like the longing for sleep after a tiring day—cutting seems more like a need than a want. In her chilling and tragically vulnerable memoir *Skin Game*, Caroline Kettlewell expresses, "I needed to cut the way your lungs scream for air when you swim the length of the pool underwater in one breath. It was a craving so organic it seemed to have arisen from my skin itself."[2]

A quick note on the subject of thoughts that "just come to" people: It may seem instinctive to assume that these thoughts always indicate spiritual oppression. Certainly the Enemy plays a major role in the introduction of destructive ideas. But jumping to the conclusion that the problem is primarily or only spiritual in nature can actually hinder the healing of a self-harmer who needs to confront any physical imbalances that should be corrected, as well as past experiences that may have caused him or her to fuse self-nurturing and self-wounding impulses.

Despite their good intentions, people who counsel self-injurers to pray their problems away and read the Bible more or those who assume every self-harmer needs a demon exorcised from him or her (this actually happened to a self-wounding friend of mine, and it devastated her) do no service to understanding the complex nature of self-injury.

On the other hand, those who claim that self-injury has nothing to do with the spirit and rely strictly on techniques for self-improvement often find that the complex and flawed nature of humanity cannot provide an anchor of hope strong enough to endure. Systems of self-improvement can accomplish some things. But they can never answer all the questions of suffering.

The idea to wound themselves "just pops into" people's heads because the human soul, body, and psyche are mysteriously and simultaneously broken and powerful. Again, encouraging self-harmers to address all aspects of healing is the only path toward full recovery.

Another group of self-harmers don't consciously decide to self-injure; rather, they stumble upon self-inflicted violence "by accident." Gabby, a bright and attractive college student, shared her story as an example of this. Gabby excelled in almost every area of life, but academic achievement remained her special glory—she was the first in her family to graduate from high school and go on to college. When she arrived at the university, however, she felt, well, *average.* And average was not okay for Gabby. Throughout the first semester, her tension built until it hit ferocious levels. Digging long, manicured fingernails into her hands one day in class, Gabby noticed that the pressure had drawn blood from her palm. But what startled her more than the bleeding cut was the fact that she felt soothed by the sight of her wounded hand.

Before that day, Gabby had never entertained a conscious thought about hurting herself. According to her, it just "happened." It also worked. When anxiety threatened Gabby again, she remembered the relief that injuring herself had unleashed, and she chose to self-wound again . . . and again.

"Accidental" self-harmers like Gabby often report that their self-inflicted violence happened "automatically." A young man named Blake, whose anger at the world eventually turned inward, offers this information about his first experience with self-injury: "I was hopeless and full of rage. I started to light up a cigarette. Next thing I knew, I was plunging the hot metal of the lighter into my arm. The burn didn't even hurt. It felt clean and pure. And I was instantly calmer. Burning felt like opening a safety valve for my pain."

When humans unexpectedly discover that something relieves tension or pain, they will likely return to the method when frustration or sadness threatens again.

I also experienced this accidental discovery of self-injury when I "stumbled" on to excessive exercise as a teenager. When I started running, I couldn't believe how much the fabled "runner's high" did for my flagging spirits or pent-up anger. Unfortunately, combining increasingly disordered eating habits with my obsessive, perfectionistic personality, I began to depend on the endorphins released during intense exercise. Even when I risked knee trouble and severe shin splints, I continued in a self-harming pattern of exercise. It took time to undo the pattern that I had discovered unintentionally.

And then there are those who "learn" self-injury. When people observe a behavior that seems satisfying and rewarding for others, they often replicate the act. Scientists call this observational learning.

This dangerous type of observational learning seems to be a particular problem among adolescents. While teenagers may act aloof or obsessively secretive around adults, they often play a whole different ball game among their peers. Instead of concealing the behavior they hide from parents or authority figures, many self-harming teens "educate" each other—in gory detail—about how their self-injurious practices work. The media certainly doesn't help teens in this predicament.

In psychiatric hospitals, prisons, boarding schools, group homes, or similar facilities, lack of privacy combined with a high population of residents unaccustomed to dealing with intense emotion can lead to a contagious outbreak of self-injury.

Teenagers living in emotionally impoverished environments (which can also be a common experience in institutional settings) may receive special attention (albeit usually negative in nature) because of their engagement in self-harm. Sadly, this reinforces self-wounding behavior. Their logic seems to be this: If people are ignored or treated derisively until they inflict violence on themselves, why wouldn't they continue to inflict harm in hopes of receiving more attention?

Consider this: If you "just came up" with the idea of self-injury, if you stumbled on to it by accident, or if you discovered it by watching someone else find comfort in it, once it worked for you, do you think you might be tempted to continue the behavior?

HOW DO PEOPLE INJURE THEMSELVES?

Virtually anything can be used as a tool to inflict harm on the body. Many parents or loved ones who discover that someone is self-wounding attempt to remove potentially dangerous implements from the self-harmer's home and workplace. But these same people quickly find that household items, school supplies, or clothing accessories can all turn into weapons.

You simply cannot remove every "unsafe" article from a person's life. A discarded tin can, an eraser, or the clasp of a watch can become tools for self-inflicted violence. In the adolescent novel *Cut*, a hardened, cynical self-injurer named Amanda recalls, "I knew a girl who used her father's credit card. Nice touch. Little hidden psychological message in that, don't you think?"[3]

Self-injurers can be incredibly creative and persistent, using whatever they can until they find relief. And while some are impulsive, many plan out elaborate rituals to inflict violence on themselves. They use "significant" instruments (perhaps the same tool over and over or something with a painful emotional connection). Self-harmers often wound themselves in the same places and at certain times of the day (for instance, in the bathroom, while showering before bed). Patterns like these do not develop by accident. Controlled and carefully routinized, like the very act of self-inflicted violence itself, these patterns serve a specific and significant purpose for the sufferer.

On a positive note, the sometimes ritualistic nature of self-injury can actually benefit those who want to help. Since seclusion and privacy are often required for routine-driven self-harmers to feel "safe" enough to wound themselves, simply being with a self-injurer during a particularly difficult time of day or through a painful situation can significantly decrease the likelihood of self-inflicted violence. Also, the feelings of alienation and isolation that compel people to self-wound may diminish in the presence of someone who loves and supports them.

Kelly Campbell, a nineteen-year-old college student, recently told *WORLD* magazine about her daily self-injurious routine. The article explains, "After her last class, she would return to her room, run a safety pin under water, and begin slicing her left arm—usually between the elbow and wrist. . . . She also devised several 'rules': 'If I made one cut, I had to make three and they had to be even. If I made a cut above my elbow I had to use an X-Acto blade and it had to be in a straight line. I never made a cut twice on the same place.'"[4]

If you were one of Kelly's friends or family members, offering to stay with her after class would likely break her self-wounding routine. And even challenging her to go against her own "rules" if she did give in to the urge to cut could helpfully disrupt her pattern.

I realize that when you desperately want someone to stop self-harming, it may seem ridiculous to counsel him or her to make one cut instead of three. But as with every deeply entrenched pattern, small steps are significant ones. Breaking the "rules" would make Kelly's self-injury less satisfying. And when a behavior leads to disappointment rather than gratification, it often proves easier to stop.

Others like Philip, a young man who allowed his therapist to write about his battle with self-harm, present specific problems because they naturally gravitate to impulsive behaviors.[5] Philip reported that he picks his skin in uncomfortable settings but does not realize what he's been doing until his skin breaks and blood runs. As it did for Philip, impulsivity and a lack of self-awareness may make controlling self-inflicted violence more difficult for the people you love.

But difficult does not mean impossible. Once self-injurers like Philip recognize their patterns and the things/situations/people that trigger them to begin self-wounding, recovery is that much closer. Many compulsive self-harmers also discover physiological causes for their obsessive and recurrent actions. This will be discussed further in forthcoming chapters.

A final note on how people can wound themselves. Many concerned loved ones wonder if tattooing and piercing fall into the self-injury category. I'm quite sure that any number of parents would testify that their son or daughter's body modification certainly appears self-harming.

Even so, we cannot make blanket statements about the relationship between "body art" and self-inflicted violence. Rather, we can recognize that a continuum exists here, a continuum that ranges from the innocuous to the destructive.

In general, the motives behind body modification determine where an individual's tattooing or piercing falls on that continuum. For people who pursue multiple tattoos or piercings because they feel "high" when the needle pricks their skin, the behavior is closer to self-harm than it is for those who see them as a relatively "safe" (meaning unmotivated by the narcotic effect of the process itself) means of artistic expression.

If you suspect someone you love uses body modification to avoid emotional pain or to alter his or her state of being, the best way to confirm or deter your suspicions is to begin a dialogue with him or her. Observing patterns and listening to the vocabulary he or she uses will also help. Through it all, leaning on God for wisdom and discernment is, as in all things, the best place to start.

IT'S NOT THAT MUCH DIFFERENT FROM WHAT YOU MAY DO

Allow me to set the record straight on one important issue: People who self-harm are not psycho, deranged, or weird. They certainly are not "freaks." Like all of us, self-injurers are trying to make sense of a pain-ridden, broken existence. Those who choose self-inflicted violence as a means of controlling and finding relief from unmanageable sadness or anguish are *not* crazy.

Many of us know people who abuse alcohol, drowning their sorrows in a fifth of scotch. We ache watching friends overeat or undereat, vomit, or exercise obsessively in an effort to avoid emotional pain. And though it may be a less obvious method of "morbid self-help," thousands of people, many of them God-fearing men and women, try to shop, work, or even serve their problems away.

The feelings that drive us to faulty—and often sinful—coping mechanisms are common to all people. Fear, anger, confusion, overwhelming memories or circumstances, abandonment, rejection, loss of control or the fear of it, failed trust, and broken relationships plague every single one of us at one time or another. The wounds inflicted on us by others, the sins we choose, and the attacks of our soul's Enemy leave all of us with a choice: How will we cope?

Our problems are further compounded by the reality that every human starts life needy and ill-equipped to face the onslaught of pain that living on earth entails. We all learn coping mechanisms, and many of the methods we use to care for ourselves are laced with sin and shame.

We all have experienced feelings that threaten to overwhelm us. This is true: The self-injurer you love is more like you than you may imagine. You both fear. You both have felt hopeless. You both have found some way to face life.

And whether a person heads to the gym or the casino; seeks relief in food, drug, or drink; works overtime; shops the time away; or cuts his or her own skin, any method of dealing with pain can become dangerously harmful.

I don't know whether or not your coping mechanism is healthy and holy. But I know that every one of us has been and is continually tempted to protect the self, escape pain, and numb ourselves to that which could destroy us.

Recognizing that the person who self-injures is not all that different from me gave me renewed vision for each self-harmer's dignity. Rather than shaking my head in confusion and frustration, I began to feel genuine compassion for those who feel pain, just as I do, who need hope, just as I do, and who use broken means to find relief, just like I do. But I still wanted to know more about why people turn to self-inflicted violence instead of any number of other things.

EXPLORING WHAT WE'VE BEEN HINTING AT

Now that we have an explanation of the act itself, an understanding of how a pattern begins, and the terminology to describe self-inflicted violence, it's time to further investigate the many reasons people start and continue to self-wound. To begin, though, I'd like to describe what self-injury is *not*.

Self-harm is not a failed suicide attempt.

Remember, self-injury can be described as a form of self-help and a wounding embrace. People who engage in self-inflicted violence are usually not trying to end their lives; instead, they are attempting to find temporary relief from their pain. Self-injury is most often used as a survival technique rather than an exit strategy.

Sufferers may entertain thoughts about suicide. And some habitual self-wounders do try to take their own lives. We'll delve into that a bit more in the next chapter. But for right now, it's essential to note that this is not *why* people—even those who think about or attempt suicide—cut or burn or hurt themselves in other ways.

Instead, a common refrain among self-harmers is, "I felt I'd die if I didn't cut." Self-inflicted violence, rather than a suicide attempt, is often a last-ditch effort to grab hold of life, however painful that life may be.

Self-wounders also view their actions as a way to "reset" their life, to take it down to a baseline from which they can rebuild a better, safer self. Most self-harmers don't want to kill *themselves* but something *in* themselves—pain, fear, anger, feelings of worthlessness, and so on.

Self-injury is not a "girl's problem."

Despite what I once believed and what you may have heard, self-inflicted violence is not something only girls deal with. According to Dr. Tracy Alderman, the proportion of men and women who engage in self-inflicted violence is roughly equal.[6] Men and women do, however, seem to deal with their self-injurious tendencies in different ways. When comparing male and female self-harmers, the following patterns become evident.

Men tend to seek psychiatric or psychotherapeutic care less often than women do. Because much of what we know about psychological issues comes from these disciplines, women are sometimes more readily identified as potential and current self-injurers.

In addition, men sometimes minimize or rationalize away mental-health conditions. Yet as Dr. Wendy Lader and Karen Conterio, directors of the S.A.F.E. (Self-Abuse Finally Ends) Alternatives program in Illinois, note, "Just because men mask their vulnerability doesn't mean it isn't there. Indeed, if you looked at the intake questionnaires that all patients fill out when they arrive at S.A.F.E. and covered up the names, you would never be able to tell the men from the women."[7] When life hurts, men turn as often as women do to self-injurious behaviors.

But men also tend toward outward displays of violence and others-focused harm. That is why men with mental instabilities often end up in prisons, while chemically imbalanced women more frequently show up in psychiatric institutions.

Self-injury is not a "teenage problem" that people simply outgrow.

In their study of 240 habitual self-harmers, Armando Favazza and Karen Conterio describe a "typical" female self-injurer: a twenty-eight-year-old Caucasian who first started deliberately self-wounding at age fourteen. She has injured herself on at least fifty occasions (though many self-harmers may injure themselves this many times in a single year or less). She now has or has had an eating disorder and may be concerned about her drinking. She also has been a heavy utilizer of medical and mental-health services, although treatment generally has been unsatisfactory.[8]

While this "typical" self-injurer began harming herself at fourteen, she has continued well into adulthood. The number of her injuries is staggering, and she clearly has not "grown out" of her disorder. In fact, eating issues as well as possible substance abuse have been added to the mix. And medical treatment, though "heavily utilized" has not benefited her.

No similar study has been performed on a population of male self-harmers, but from everything I have read and observed, the pattern would likely prove strikingly similar.

Before we all start hyperventilating, imagining our friend or child in this condition, remember that the point of this book is that there is hope and healing. The story of redemption is real.

But it's important to acknowledge that this profile could become anyone we love. Do not ignore warning signs and assume that "this teenage stuff will sort itself out." Self-injury, whether infrequent or obsessively repetitive, is not a problem to dismiss as adolescent nonsense that will go away with time.

Many people associate self-harm with the troubled teen, the black-wearing, moody, and angry young person who lashes out at everyone, including himself or herself. This may describe some self-harmers, to be sure, but a picture like this reveals only one piece in the mosaic of self-injurious personalities.

PhDs and high-school dropouts, homeless and fabulously wealthy people (like Princess Diana) use self-inflicted violence to numb or escape pain. Individuals from every race and nation suffer in silent self-hate. People in high-profile positions — professors, lawyers, engineers, even doctors and therapists — have confessed to acts of self-injury. Some are perfectionists; others are incredibly depressed.

Physical pain is not the point of self-injury.
Self-harmers usually do not *enjoy* the physical pain they feel. Listen to the enlightening words of one self-injurer: "It's never about liking

pain. If I liked pain, then it wouldn't help. I hate it. That's why it helps. . . . I feel terrible. I have to make my feelings go away. I [just] use very bitter medicine to make them go away."[9]

Some self-injurers describe hurting themselves as an out-of-body experience, where someone else wields the blade and feels the pain. Others say they don't feel pain while self-injuring because what they ultimately want is to feel better. It's mind over matter. For them, any pain that comes is a path to peace, not only bearable but often emotionally pleasurable.

Another important variable in the self-wounding equation seems to be personal control over the injury (including any physical sensations that come with it): Self-harmers want to be the ones to decide when and how they get hurt. They also want to manage and be able to savor the physical and emotional benefits of the act. Emily, a sixteen-year-old receiving treatment at the Two Brattle Center, reports, "When I would cut myself deliberately, I didn't even feel it. . . . But if I got a paper cut I didn't want, that would hurt."[10]

The ironic truth is that many people who self-wound use pain to erase pain.

———

I hope debunking a few common myths about self-injury has helped you, as it did me. Now let's look more intently at why people choose self-injury to face life's pains and problems. In the following section, we will review and introduce new ideas. By more explicitly listing some potential motivations for self-wounding, I think we can synthesize the things we've already begun to learn, as well as those we haven't yet discussed.

THE TIP OF AN ICEBERG

Self-injury is symptomatic of a deeper emotional, spiritual, and often physical problem. Cutting or burning are behaviors that form the tip of an iceberg, an iceberg that goes deep within a person's heart and soul.

If we truly desire to come alongside someone who self-harms, we must see beyond the symptoms, beyond the shocking and often frightening actions. We must see a person, not a disorder.

Steven Levenkron writes, "Self-mutilation is a frightening barrier that keeps us from seeing a person who is lost, in pain, and in desperate need of help."[11]

No self-wounder is the sum of his or her symptoms. To show people we care, we can avoid labeling in simplistic, dismissive ways. We can listen to the complex and rich stories of hurting people. When we listen to the pain that prompts people to self-injure, we find empathy for their choice to use this coping mechanism.

I questioned whether or not to list the reasons that individuals self-wound because putting something at the top of a list might indicate it is the most important, or most common, reason. Again, allow me to reassert that there simply isn't *one* answer for the question "Why?" In fact, most self-injurers cut or burn or break bones for several of the following reasons. Others don't know exactly why they self-harm, but they resonate with a number of these ideas. With that in mind, let's look at some ways self-wounders have responded to the question "Why?"

"It works."

One of the most rudimentary, but also prevailing and powerful, reasons people self-wound is because *it works*.

Self-inflicted violence is an incredibly powerful, effective, and intoxicatingly immediate way to relieve tension. Physical pain, the visual stimulation of blood or burns, and the relief that comes efficiently distract people from emotions or circumstances they do not want to — or feel they cannot — face.

It takes only a moment to hurt yourself. For many, relief instantaneously floods the mind and body. Self-injury, quite simply, gets the job done.

"I need a way to 'release' pain."

We've discussed this a bit, but let's review briefly: All of us release tension in some way. We laugh. We cry. We may pound the pavement on a hard-core run. We may scream or lash out at others. Some people wound themselves.

In the piercing words of one self-injurer, "There are times when I just hurt too bad—too deep for tears—so I cut and it lets out some of the hurt. . . . It's like when you see the blood flowing out, the pain and fear are flowing out with it. Or at least I want them to."[12]

For most of us, tears or rage (not blood or burns) are the body's language for pain. Crying serves both physiological and psychological functions, effectively releasing sorrow. Lashing out in anger, while typically an unhealthier means of release than crying, also acts as a physical and emotional outlet for grief.

But self-harmers on the whole "are either too numb to cry or find tears woefully inadequate to express and release the overwhelming, pent-up emotions they feel."[13] As another self-injurer writes, "I need to see [the] bad feelings bleed away. . . . I couldn't cry, and bleeding was a different form of crying."[14]

"I couldn't handle it all."

People with chronically ill or unemployed family members, children of addicts, and those with emotionally or physically absent and/or abusive caregivers may sense that they have no one to lean on, no one to take care of them. A security or authority void (often a combination of both) can cause a breakdown in the family, which results in children prematurely and inappropriately assuming adult roles and responsibilities.

The stresses of unemployment, chronic illness, or physical impairment can cause a role reversal that makes children susceptible to a number of unhealthy behaviors, including self-injury. Absent or emotionally unavailable caregivers, as well as family members who deliberately hurt each other, can also trigger feelings of continuous endangerment and profound vulnerability. This proves particularly true when parents under personal or career duress look to their children for emotional reassurance and validation, even financial support.

Raised in homes like these, children often struggle to survive, and they receive the message that they must look out for themselves. Desperate to establish order, they may create pervasive rituals so they can depend on something, anything. Routinized acts may range from obsessive care for other family members to disordered eating and habitual self-inflicted violence.

Tragically, abused and neglected children, especially those of alcoholics or mentally disturbed parents, often find themselves "in charge" of maintaining the physical and emotional stability of the family. Not only do they lack the psychological maturity to face the challenges in their home, but they also have been taught few or no skills to do even the things they should be able to do at their age.

Swiss psychologist Alice Miller, author of *Prisoners of Childhood*, describes with heartbreaking eloquence the devastating consequences of childhood abuse and neglect. She explains that when parents intentionally harm or ignore their children, or when emotional dysfunctions make parents ill-prepared to support their families, children learn to subordinate their needs to those of the abusive or neglectful parents.

These children cut off and then lock away their true selves—their need for love and understanding, along with the angry and resentful feelings they have—in what Miller calls an inner prison. Emptiness, hopelessness, and bitterness continue to hold many people captive to their childhood pain. Some will cut to keep the feelings at bay; others will burn to feel anything but the numb deadness they've lived with as long as they can remember.

Other parents fail to consider the ages and maturity levels of their children, trying to communicate with them in inappropriately adult ways. People who feel like they don't have or never had a childhood may self-injure out of the pressure and confusion of role reversal. They don't want to make all the decisions. They don't want to be the emotional barometer for their family.

The bottom line is that children need their parents to be parents. They need to be kids. Thankfully, confused familial roles are not irreversible, especially if appropriately faced and dealt with. As children feel more secure in their homes and in their roles, they may cease "needing" self-injury as an outlet for their feelings.

"I just wanted to feel something, anything."

As you may have picked up on, self-wounders may feel alternately, or all at once, agonizingly pained and completely numb. "Am I really here?," "Is this what it means to be alive?," and "Can anyone see me?" are common questions among self-harmers. A young girl who identifies herself online as "Happy #" expresses, "The greatest loss in life is not death. It's what dies inside while you['re] alive."

Self-injurers sometimes say that they cut to feel "alive" or "real." They fight emotional deadness by cutting or burning, assuring themselves they can still feel. For them, sensing pain is sometimes better than feeling nothing at all.

Self-inflicted violence involves strong physical stimuli, and hurting people sometimes think they *need* such tactile responses of the body in order to feel alive. Others literally believe they *need* the visual stimulus of watching their blood flow or their flesh burn to stay connected to reality.

"The wounds make my infinite pain (temporarily) finite."

Psychologist Dan Allender explains that intense anguish dispels all thoughts other than the desire for relief. And Caroline Kettlewell describes how cutting spun the chaos in her head "into a silk of silence." She found cutting distilled herself to "the immediacy of hand, blade, blood, flesh."[15]

When people experience deep hurts that seem vague, undefined, and never ending, they naturally seek a way to end the agony. In order to control hurt that seems infinite, self-harmers often create physical pain, which is finite, and physical wounds, which eventually heal.

"I just feel so alone."

Self-injurers often speak of alienation and isolation plaguing them. They fear being alone and can feel desperately lonely even when others are present. Whether alienated from family, other nurturing adults, or peers, men and women sometimes use self-inflicted violence in an effort to hold feelings of isolation at bay. The loneliness that comes in the wake of a divorce provides a heartbreaking example of an isolating circumstance that may precipitate self-injurious behavior.

After a divorce, children and spouses often feel abandoned, outraged, and angry at everyone and anyone for letting them down. Many children stop looking to their parents as moral authorities. Furiously wounded, they may — through self-wounding behavior — scream, "How dare you tell me what to do when you've screwed everything up?"

Some self-injurers watch their parents and learn only distorted things about relationships. The strongest messages are that nobody really loves anybody, you'd better take what you can get, and love doesn't last forever.

Children often feel unable to face the pain of their parents' split. Lydia's story vividly communicates how divorce can play a part in self-injury:

My parents went through an incredibly messy, painful divorce after I turned twelve. I used to get calls from my mom, claiming I didn't love her because I wanted to live with my dad. Now I know that she has her own problems to deal with, but at the time it was too much for me.

I would burst out in tears for "no reason." Irrational, inexplicable fears started to crop up. First I couldn't sleep by a window; then I couldn't stay the night in my own bedroom. The dark terrified me. Until my sister moved in with my dad and me, I slept in a little bed in my dad's room.

One day, I shut myself in the bathroom, climbed into the bathtub, and sobbed for what seemed like forever. I spotted the razor. Everything raged and ached within me. It was too painful to handle everything by myself.

The razor cut me. Or rather, I cut myself using the razor. But, you know, it sort of felt like someone else was doing it. I had never even heard about self-injury. If memory serves, the idea had never crossed my mind before that moment. The first cut just happened.

For some time, the smallest conflict with my mom or dad could send me spiraling with defeat and anger, fear and hurt. My emotions would build and build until I couldn't deal anymore. Then I would cut. It always happened when I felt really overwhelmed. Sometimes days, even weeks, would pass before the impulse to cut returned.

Before I cut, while I cut, after I cut, I cried and cried. I wouldn't even have been able to tell you exactly why. Everything was just so confusing that tears and pain were the only way that I ever felt a release.

And I never wanted anyone to find out. It was a dirty secret, something I couldn't control. I would try to not even think about it. The shame hurt almost as much as my parents' split. I had a list of excuses in case anyone discovered my slices or scars. Every time I cut, regret plagued me, but stopping seemed impossible. Admitting that I depended on hurting myself seemed even more frightening.

The only thing that helped me was talking to God. Not just praying, but talking to God like I would talk to a friend. I could cry out to God when I couldn't even express myself to anyone else. Ultimately, I found it easier to turn everything over to God instead of trying to sort things out in my head.

Slowly, the cutting became more and more sporadic. I didn't need to inflict pain to feel better like I used to. Years later, I'm self-injury free. Things like your parents' splitting never "go away," but learning to face and deal with my feelings about it helped make the pain bearable.

People who feel isolated from peers confirm that expressing need or uncomfortable emotions to others (who may reject them) seems virtually impossible; sadly, this often causes them to sink into their loneliness even further. Others cling to any relationships—including tremendously destructive ones—simply because being with someone, no matter how harmful, feels better than being alone.

As family members and friends recognize the ways in which separation from loved ones or from peers affects self-injurers, self-inflicted violence may become less of a "necessary" coping method. Communication, family togetherness, and the development of an individual's unique place in a community can begin to replace the isolating emotions that often lead to self-injury.

"I can't say it any other way."

In her book *The Body Project*, Joan Jacobs Brumberg claims that many young women today regard their bodies as message boards.[16] Men often use their bodies in a similar manner. The way a person dresses, uses makeup, and/or modifies the body often signals much more than taste or artistic preference.

Men and women who self-injure often see their bodies as their *only* message board, their best method of communication. Self-inflicted violence makes audible their silent shrieks within.

A close friend of mine who battled self-harm for more than three years once cut lines that looked like teardrops on her face. For Charity, this tragic representation of deep anguish seemed not only reasonable but the right way to express her pain.

When self-harmers claim they have "no other way to express what they feel," they often speak truth. In their current impoverished repertoire of coping skills and modes of communication, self-inflicted violence is the most powerful—in the worst cases, the *only*—tool they know how to use. The next point relates closely to this one.

"Self-injury makes my invisible pain visible."

William Shakespeare once declared,

> My grief lies all within;
> And these external manners of laments

Are merely shadows to the unseen grief
That swells with silence in the tortured soul.[17]

People who inflict wounds on the body often speak of needing their inner pain to "show on the outside." Self-injury is a way to make deep emotional distress definite, not only to others but also to the self-harmer. Self-inflicted violence brings the shadows of unseen grief that swell in a tortured soul to physical expression.

In this way, self-harm certainly acts as a potent form of communication, but tragically, its messages often are misinterpreted. Self-inflicted violence communicates pain but in an extraordinarily indirect fashion. The meaning behind a recently inflicted wound may be misread or distorted by others, even those who long to understand.

In the worst scenarios, a cry for help is misunderstood as a manipulative act. People may actually avoid a self-injurer, frustrated because they have misinterpreted his or her signs. Yet most self-wounders don't intend to manipulate but to authentically communicate.

Self-injurious messages often run along these lines:

- I need help.
- I don't know what else to do.
- I feel lost and alone.
- I would like someone to help care for me.

I like the differentiation Jan Sutton makes between "attention-needing" and "attention-seeking." She claims that self-injurers rarely use their self-destructive behavior simply to get attention; instead, they are indicating a desperate need for it.[18]

The difficult reality remains, however, that certain problems can be exacerbated by too much attention. For instance, children may have learned from an early age that expressing their needs in desperate ways (for example, "I'm going to kill myself if you do/don't _____") really gets people to sit up and take notice. Is a threat like this serious or part of an acting-out fit?

Unfortunately, there are no surefire ways to know. You can, however, piece together other clues from your loved one's behavior to determine if he or she is attention-seeking or attention-needing.

A suicide threat is always serious, but coming from a person who evidences no other self-destructive practices, it may communicate the need for boundaries rather than your frantic attention. On the other hand, if your loved one has adopted a self-injurious practice, it's likely a sign that your attention, or the attention of someone else he or she loves, is desperately needed. As with many life issues, navigating situations like this requires discernment and patience.

If someone you love appears to be using self-inflicted violence as a means of communication, try using open-ended, nonthreatening questions to explore together what his or her self-harm really means. You can turn to appendix D for some examples.

Asking a self-injurer to journal about or even start verbalizing the answers to questions such as these may be helpful: "If your wounds could speak, what would they say?," "Is there someone in particular your hurts would communicate with?," and "How would you like the messages you're sending to be received?" At an appropriate time, you may also share the ways you have interpreted or are interpreting this self-harmer's expressions of pain.

Keep in mind that genuine needs will remain unmet if miscommunication persists. Both you and the self-injurer, however, can actively work against the forces of misunderstanding that often perpetuate destructive behaviors.

"I need to control something."

Self-inflicted violence often starts during adolescence, which is a time of radical change and turmoil. As teenagers strive to assert their independence, cope with their developing bodies, and redefine their relationships as young adults, they often feel the need to control and bring stability to any area of life that they can.

For adolescents who view the world as chaotic and hostile, self-harm is one means of establishing autonomy. When people injure themselves, they often do so in an effort to control uncontrollable circumstances.

Many self-harmers find themselves in a world that not only *feels* harsh and confusing but actually *is* extraordinarily antagonistic. For the abused, for the deeply anxious or depressed, for the child who loses a parent to death or alcoholism, the need for control increases dramatically during adolescence.

Even for seemingly "well-adjusted" teens, insecure peer relationships and academic or spiritual pressure may spark the use of extreme coping mechanisms such as self-inflicted violence.

And though the onset of self-injury usually comes during the turbulent adolescent years, it often peaks during the early to midtwenties, another period of tremendous change and challenge.

As people navigate college and the launch of a career, adolescent-like self-doubt and conflict reassert themselves. In our twenties, we confront a host of unfamiliar responsibilities. During this time, those who have used self-inflicted violence in the past, as well as those who discovered it recently, may self-harm to manage insecurity, pain, and tension.

Self-wounders, like all of us, prefer to be in control of their pain and their numbness. Tragically, they choose a maladaptive means of attaining temporary control.

"I had to quiet my racing thoughts."

Self-inflicted violence may also be used to relieve the tension of uncontrollable, unruly thoughts. Caroline Kettlewell speaks of her need to silence the shrieking rabble in her head, the thoughts that screeched, "*Whatareyougoingtodowhatareyougoingtodowhatareyougoingtodo?*"[19]

Typical thoughts that plague self-injurers may sound like these:

- I'm a complete idiot! I'm such a disgrace!
- How stupid can I be?
- What a screwup I am!

- I am so ugly.
- I can't believe how fat I am.
- My life sucks . . .
- And you know what? It's never going to get better.
- Nobody loves me. I must be unlovable.

We've all experienced the power of an obsessive thought. When a consumingly wonderful feeling (like falling in love) or a terribly oppressive feeling (like wondering if that lump means cancer) overcomes us, we've all seen how space in our mind for other thoughts shrinks considerably.

Self-harmers substitute thoughts about hurting themselves—and then add the act of self-inflicted violence itself—to deflect negative thought patterns. Pushing aside obsessive thoughts with focused, if self-wounding, ones *does* work. Sadly, people often find it more effective, and definitely more immediate, than healthier methods of processing distressing thoughts and feelings.

It's undeniably true: Physical sensations and behaviors can alter our state of consciousness. If you inadvertently cut yourself, thoughts about your failed business meeting or class project probably fade, at least for a moment. Some self-injurers repeatedly create this kind of physical "crisis" to control intrusive, pessimistic thoughts.

"I wanted to prove I really am hurting."
Robert, a twenty-year-old artist who uses cigarettes to burn himself, articulates, "I have a hard time talking about what's going on inside me. When I start talking, all of the crap I'm saying sounds so lame. I like looking at the scars on my arms because I know that they're real. It's like I'm trying to say, I've suffered, man, just look."[20]

Many self-harmers doubt their ability to evaluate their own emotions. Some have been told that their feelings don't matter or are invalid; others have never been taught how to discern between appropriate and inappropriate emotional expressions. Whatever the case, self-injurers often report that they want to verify internal hurts through physical acts.

An online poet, C. Blount, beautifully and pointedly illuminates this:

> How will you know I'm hurting
> If you cannot see my pain?
> To wear it on my body
> Tells what words cannot explain[21]

"I have to show I'm 'tough enough.'"

Other self-injurers wound themselves not to display their emotional turmoil but rather to show they are *immune* to pain. They can handle it. They can take it. They are strong enough. Or so they may like you to think.

Consider Jason's authoritative but tragic words: "I didn't know why I cut myself for a long time; all I knew was that it hurt but I really couldn't stop myself. I liked the pain, because it meant that I was strong. Strong enough to overcome my own natural instinct to avoid pain, and strong enough to endure the pain without crying out."[22]

Some self-harmers claim that it's "brave," even "cool," to endure pain. But this bravado usually disguises unaddressed rage or deep insecurity. In order to truly assist the Jasons we know, we'll need to explore questions like, "Where does true strength come from?" I hope we can do that together in the chapters focused on treatment and recovery.

"It purified me."

For those who view themselves as "bad" or "damaged," as well as for perfectionists who feel the need to punish themselves after every mistake, self-injury provides a way to prove they are sorry for anything they have done wrong.

As we previously noted, self-harmers often speak of the need to "get rid of bad blood" or "burn/cut the evil out of themselves." Some express that when they self-injure, they feel "clean" and "bare." Others articulate that they can "start over" after they show how sorry they are for doing or feeling something "bad."

They may also feel that they "deserve" punishment. Perhaps that was or is communicated to them at home; perhaps they have an overblown sense of personal failure. In either case, people often feel the need to say they're sorry for mistakes or wrongs committed. The most effective and potent way they know to do this is by deliberately hurting themselves.

"It gave me an excuse to take care of myself."

Self-wounders often report that they never learned to nurture, look after, or love themselves. The only time some self-harmers receive caring attention is when they are physically injured (whether accidental or as a result of intentional abuse). Almost all self-harmers have discovered that the aching chaos inside is much harder to face than the external wounds they can create.

A cut or a burn is far easier to treat than a psychological or emotional injury. A careful cleansing ritual, a gently applied ointment and bandage often serve a dual purpose: to meet the physical need presented by a fresh wound, as well as to postpone the pressing need to confront amorphous internal pain. Ironically, self-injury can be used to both punish and nurture the self.

"For me, love means pain."

Self-inflicted violence may also provide a way for the formerly abused to reenact pain from their childhood. The experience of one of Steven Levenkron's patients, a young woman named Tracy, illuminates this truth.[23]

When she was growing up, Tracy's father lived up to the title "mean drunk." No matter what she did, her dad found fault with it. During his frequent inebriated rages, Tracy's father would lash her with a belt. The heavy metal buckle often tore the skin on her arms and back. After each painful episode, Tracy's dad apologized profusely. He showered her with affectionate words and touch. For Tracy, pain and love literally bled into one another.

During Tracy's teenage years, her father stopped the abuse. But as the lashings ceased, the little bits of affection Tracy had clung to also disappeared. One day, Tracy used the very belt her dad had cruelly wounded her with to slice her own skin. It was her only hope, a desperate cry for love.

This is an incredibly difficult idea for most of us to grasp. We imagine that if we suffered abuse, we would run from and avoid anything reminiscent of that pain. In reality, however, many victims of abuse, like Tracy, find security and injury, love and pain fused in an inextricable, horrible way.

When physical, verbal, or sexual pain guides people through the most formative years of their lives, wounds become a familiar part of "home." In fact, self-injurers may trust *only* their pain, because that is their one steady, if impoverished, connection with relationship and "love." Self-inflicted violence embraces pain and even *reenacts* it because it feels right and (as ironic as this seems to us) safe.

Conversely, reenacting abuse allows some self-injurers to control the outcome, to reverse the love-equals-pain equation. When self-harmers choose to mete out "manageable" doses of pain, they often do so to redefine a situation in which they initially had little, if any, control. In this way, self-injurers can play the role of both abused *and* abuser, thus overturning, if only momentarily, the helplessness of their experience.

Some people carry burdens of extreme guilt connected with their abuse. Perhaps abusive parents told their children that the abuse was their fault or that if they were really sorry, the abuse would stop. Perhaps sensations of physical pleasure accompanied sexual abuse. Violent, self-punishing acts often spring from feelings and perceptions like these.

Finally, some former (or current) victims of abuse self-injure during physically altered states caused by dissociation, flashbacks, and post-traumatic stress disorder. Due to the complexity of these physiological conditions, we will explore these situations in forthcoming chapters.

CAN PEOPLE GET BETTER?

After reading this chapter, I hope you can see that for self-injurers, cutting or burning seems logical, perhaps inevitable. Caroline Kettlewell writes, "There's probably no critical mass beyond which cutting yourself would ever seem, to most people, . . . like a reasonable choice. I cut because it did look that way to me."[24]

We can lean in and listen to the "logic" of self-harm, or we can run and hide in fear, anger, and resignation. We can acknowledge that self-harm holds great meaning for those who do it, or we can dismiss their behavior as irrational and absurd. The decisions we make define how effective we will be in helping those we care for confront their self-inflicted violence.

Let me share with you one piece of tremendously good news: Recovery does not correlate so much with the severity or frequency of self-injurious acts as it does with the presence of ongoing support, vigorous and committed pursuit of care (including follow-through with plans laid out by professionals), and a willingness to look at one's self, family, and coping mechanisms openly and honestly.

You may fear that you or the people you love will never get through this. They've used self-injury too long. They've wounded themselves too severely. They're too far along to learn anything new.

Please do not believe these debilitating lies.

You can help provide the consistent supportive network of love that self-injurers need during recovery. You can help them rigorously pursue therapy, medical attention, and self-exploration. And you can model for them honest self-evaluation and healthy coping methods.

3 MISERY LOVES COMPANY

Environmental and Physical Conditions That Often Accompany Self-Injury

——— IN MY EXPERIENCE ———

By Dr. Earl Henslin

At first glance, Joy seemed to have it all. This bright, articulate, and attractive twenty-year-old college student competed athletically for her university, worked part-time, served at her church, and maintained a high GPA in the midst of it all.

To her parents, friends, and most everyone she interacted with (especially those at church), Joy lived up to her name. But after reading my book *You Are Your Father's Daughter*, Joy made an appointment to see me. That day, she started a journey of therapy that uncovered deep pain, destructive self-injury, and eventually profound healing.

Joy came to see me because the formerly tried-and-true ways of coping she had developed—people pleasing and high achieving—weren't working like they used to. Excruciating memories of the past had begun to plague Joy, and her pain escalated daily. She still tried to perform for her adoring audience but ultimately found she could no longer live with the secret shame of compulsive bulimia, paralyzing depression, and cutting.

Joy first purged at thirteen while at winter camp with her church youth group. As occurs at many such events, all of the teenagers binged on pizza, chips, and soda. Following her best friend to the bathroom, she opened the door and immediately heard the sound of vomiting. Alarmed, Joy asked if her friend needed help. Laughing nervously, but apparently undeterred, her friend said, "Just wait. I'm not finished."

When she realized that her best friend had made herself throw up,

Joy asked why she would do that. Her friend responded with a question: "Well, don't you feel fat after all we ate?" "Of course!" Joy confessed. That night, Joy learned to purge. Quickly, any "fat" feeling translated into forced vomiting.

Two weeks later, Joy was introduced to another behavior that became devastatingly compulsive. While spending the night at a friend's house, Joy first viewed male pornography. As her friend paged through a magazine, Joy watched in disbelief and mortified shock while this girl used a pulsating machine to bring herself to climax.

Her friend explained how she had walked in on her mother one day looking at porn and masturbating with a vibrator: "At first my mom seemed kind of embarrassed. But then she taught me all about it and told me it was a normal way for women to handle their feelings." Encouraged by her friend, Joy tried it out. The wave of relief and ecstasy that washed over Joy after her first orgasm calmed her in a way she had never experienced.

Before too long, however, the release she felt either in binging and purging or self-pleasuring dissipated into an uncontrollable horror. Joy masturbated and vomited compulsively, sometimes four or five times a day. She used a vibrator so often that it actually caused damage to the tissue around her sexual organs.

Late one night, overwhelmed with shame, Joy pressed a knife against her inner thigh. Self-punishing pain momentarily lifted Joy from the pit of her guilt and disgrace. She almost felt as if she had "made up for" her badness by bleeding. Cutting became yet another compulsive and self-abusive, but always secret, pattern in Joy's life.

Though I've related this story to you as an unbroken narrative, Joy had to piece her experiences together during months of therapy. And along with these confessions, memories of a severely broken relationship with her father trickled out.

At roughly the same time she was exposed to bulimia, masturbation, and cutting, Joy discovered a terrible difference between the good, public daddy she'd always adored and the private, hypocritical father that her family had known for years but neglected to warn her about.

Walking into her father's study one day, she caught this man she respected looking at pornography and masturbating. He yelled at her, "Get out . . . now!" It was too much for her. No one was who they seemed to be. Her best friend threw up regularly; another friend masturbated compulsively. Her mom passively tolerated her dad's secret sins. Joy couldn't talk to anyone about her father, let alone her life outside the family home. She vowed she would never trust again. Joy also descended into a vicious depression, one that she kept at bay only through frenetic activity and service.

These experiences cemented in her a vicious cycle of self-abuse. She raged against her body, her false dad, and the God she thought should rescue her from it all.

In session after session, Joy and I processed memories and present experiences that triggered her desire to cut, purge, and harmfully masturbate or that caused her to spiral into despair. The anger and shame of following in her father's footsteps—living a "double" life in which her private and public selves differed radically—caused Joy particular pain.

Joy had not learned from her parents the important skills of living authentically, practicing self-control, and upholding personal, including physical, respect. No one taught her how to establish and maintain boundaries. Joy never learned how to deal with complex emotions; she could translate emotional crises only into physical pain or pleasure, sometimes mixing the two in a warped attempt at self-care.

Though it took protracted and committed therapeutic work on her part, Joy was able to see glimmers of hope in her future. By learning new ways to handle pain and practicing healthier coping mechanisms rather than the tormenting ones she had become accustomed to, Joy began to experience freedom from her self-injurious behaviors.

As therapy progressed, Joy joined a mutual-help group of women who shared honestly and vulnerably with each other. They processed the pain in one another's lives and learned to bear each other's burdens. These women provided another restorative outlet for Joy. Through it all, Joy learned to confront not only cutting but disordered eating, abusive sexual expression, and depression as well.

RARELY A LONE RANGER

Self-injury does not often "travel" alone. Like Joy, many self-injurers battle one or several accompanying problems while fighting self-injurious impulses. These often include one or more of the following:

- Depression or other mood disorders
- Low self-esteem
- Eating disorders
- Parent/child conflict

- Manipulation and/or habitual lying
- Oppositional defiance
- Aggressive behavior
- Suicidal ideation
- A history of sexual abuse or present unhealthy sexual expression (including addiction to pornography or masturbation)
- Post-traumatic stress disorder
- Dissociation
- Addiction or addictive tendencies

In this chapter I'd like to address (as thoroughly as I can in limited space) several of the more common issues or situations that psychiatrists, psychotherapists, and lay counselors have observed in people who use self-inflicted violence as a coping mechanism. We'll look first at depression and other mood disorders.

DEPRESSION[1]

According to a July 2005 national women's health survey conducted by the Kaiser Family Foundation and the University of California–Los Angeles Center for Health Policy Research, nearly one in four women (23 percent) have been diagnosed with depression or anxiety.[2] And the rising incidence of depression in men has prompted the National Institute of Mental Health to create a website specifically addressing the unique ways men face depressive conditions.[3]

Yet more than two-thirds of people suffering from depression never seek treatment. Those who use self-injury in an attempt to cope with depression do so either to mitigate depressing feelings or, conversely, to be able to feel anything at all. And many people simply live with symptoms of depression, believing that their harassed emotional state is normal or a result of their own faulty living.

I have personally experienced deep and clinical depression. But even when doctors diagnosed me with a major depressive disorder, all I could think was that I had no right to be depressed. My childhood hadn't been nightmarish. Loved ones surrounded me. I had faith in God. Still, while I was "moving on the outside . . . inside [I was] slipping deep into the quicksand of alienation and isolation."[4]

When they can express emotion at all, people who cut, burn, or otherwise injure themselves use this same kind of language to describe their feelings. Words like *despair, hopelessness, emptiness*, and *apathy* frequently come up while talking with self-harmers.

"Inactivity [or overactivity], as well as difficulty in thinking and concentration"[5] also plague depressed individuals. Sufferers often feel a relentless, palpable sense of futility and worthlessness. Others feel intense, yet sometimes inexplicable, anger, hate, and bitterness.

Through the lens of deep despair, some depressed self-harmers look at the world and think, "'I am alone. No one can help me. No one cares about me.' Worse still, people stand against me. They not only avoid helping me; they try to make my life even more miserable than it is."[6]

Self-injurers may choose to wound themselves because the heartache of disappointed hopes is unbearable. They numb themselves with self-harm until all they can feel is the emptiness of depression. Since yearning for anything seems to only make them vulnerable to more pain, depressed people often shut down all desire. And this leads to a robotic existence where the heart rarely expects anything but bitterness.

It's essential to remember, however, that depression is *not* a strictly emotional condition. It affects the entire body by infecting the brain. Both the thought processes *and* systemic functioning of depressed individuals are affected.

Common symptoms of depression include interruption in sleep, appetite, and sexual cycles, and self-injurious tendencies. Depressed people's immune systems are compromised, and they may experience muscular or nerve pain. In other cases, they may feel little, if anything. And they do not create or imagine any of these conditions.

Depression also causes *and can be caused by* disturbances in the brain. Our ability to experience and participate in the world around us is made possible by the pulses of complex electrochemical activity. And just as a heart can fail to pump properly or a lung can collapse and make breathing impossible, so a brain can temporarily—or over a long period—cease to function properly, impairing a person's ability to think clearly and normally. As neurotransmitters malfunction and synapses misfire, the body receives mixed or distorted messages from the brain. A person's world can be plunged into bleak nothingness, somewhat like a television with bad reception.

And, like any of the other parts of the body, the brain may fail arbitrarily, regardless of how fortunate a person's life has been, regardless of past or present circumstances.[7]

In order to best understand depression (and self-injury, for that matter), we must view it not as an absolute quantity but as a matter of degree. Mood disorders exist on a continuum. At one extreme, we find those people with biochemical imbalances and/or severely disturbed family functioning. At the other end of the continuum, we might observe people whose present circumstances or relationships contribute to bleakness, hopelessness, and numbness.

In a fascinating way, after long periods of entertaining or experiencing feelings of intense sadness, grief, or rage, the continuum of self-harm and depression may form a full circle, plunging a person who initially experienced only circumstantial despair into full-blown chemical depression. Studying brain activity indicates that following extended exposure to toxic thought patterns, the deep limbic system—the area of the brain that helps control mood and the portion that is most affected by depression—can actually shut down.

Though it is scientifically clear that depression is both a physiological *and* cognitive condition that affects each person uniquely, some doctors write prescriptions for every patient suffering from depression, disregarding other factors that contribute to a person's well-being. Some counselors, on the other hand, downplay the importance of medication, insisting that therapy (or prayer) will eradicate depression. But research shows that most depressed individuals respond best to a combination of treatments.

We must carefully treat the despairing person's body if we are to help him or her experience peace of mind and soul. Attention to diet, sleep, and general nurturing of a person's physical condition aids in the healing process. Medication may also help.

After my first postpartum depression, I took Prozac, and the depression began to lift as soon as the drug got into my system. But, of course, medication did not (and could not) solve all my problems or erase all my fears, nor does it for any depressed individual. This is why we cannot focus *solely* on biochemical factors, neglecting the emotional and spiritual dimensions of mood disorders.

Depression influences the thoughts we hear, the ideas we confront, the state of our souls. Deep and persistent despair usually breaks down a person's sense of worth and confidence. Depression almost always undermines an individual's ability to experience pleasure in daily life, even in things he or she previously enjoyed. And it can lead to serious doubts about faith and God.

Feelings like these, whether instigated by a physiological condition or a psychological one, should not be ignored. The darkest places of the soul can be explored with the help of objective and compassionate direction. A depressed person will probably find help from either a professional or lay counselor, maybe both.

As depressed people treat both the medical and the emotional and spiritual aspects of depression, they will be changed. And amazingly, the deep-seated joy of being set free from negative thought patterns can also trigger physical reactions that literally mitigate biological symptoms.

In general, any person with undiagnosed depression and anxiety will be at greater risk for self-injurious behavior. But it's also crucial for us to recognize the connection between depression experienced by those in close relationship with a self-harmer and the self-wounder's own injurious behavior. Untreated mental sickness in parents can be a strong indicator of self-inflicted violence in children because of both genetic factors and the vacuum left by an emotionally absent parent. It's important to confront not only the despair in the self-injurer but also the physiological and emotional struggles other family members face.

ANXIETY, OBSESSION, AND IMPULSE CONTROL

Many self-harmers experience a heightened and oppressive sense of anxiety before causing themselves harm. This escalation resembles that which occurs during panic attacks. Consequently, some self-injurers may rightly receive a clinical diagnosis of anxiety disorder.

Like depression, anxiety exists on a continuum, where one extreme includes people with severe panic attacks and the other those who experience persistent, but more "common," cycles of worry.

Therapy, medication, or a combination of both can help the self-wounder who concurrently battles anxiety. If you or someone you love begins to take medication, be sure to stay informed and aware of any side effects. As mentioned in the upcoming chapter on physiology, certain anxiety medicines may increase a person's desire to inflict violence on himself or herself.

Self-harmers may also experience symptoms associated with Obsessive-Compulsive Disorder (OCD). Neurotic *To cut or not to cut? To cut or not to cut? To cut or not to cut?* thoughts can plague them. And quite often, repetitive or obsessive behaviors designed — in the sufferers' minds — to calm or erase intrusive thoughts can actually further indicate a chemical imbalance. For people who suffer from OCD, repetitive cutting or burning can become another function of compulsion.

While most self-injurers would not qualify for a clinical OCD diagnosis, *many* self-harmers experience OCD-like symptoms. The same can be true of what is identified by the Diagnostic and Statistical Manual of Mental Disorders-IV (the psychology "bible," which defines and classifies mental illnesses) as borderline personality disorder (BPD).

The DSM-IV lists self-injury as one of several possible symptoms of BPD. The others include anxiety, inappropriate anger, volatile relationships, chronic feelings of emptiness, dissociation, an imbalanced sense of self, desperate efforts to avoid real or imagined abandonment, recurrent suicidal ideation or action, and other recurrent, destructive, and impulsive behaviors.

People who struggle with BPD experience wild mood swings and emotional (often angry) outbursts. They consistently exhibit exceptionally dramatic tendencies; BPD sufferers constantly seem to be in the midst of crisis or chaos. Their high degree of impulsivity can manifest itself in reckless driving or sexual activity, excessive spending, substance abuse, and repetitive cutting, burning, or other self-injurious acts.

In relationships with others, people with BPD frequently violate boundaries, send mixed messages, hold double standards, provoke anger, and habitually manipulate or lie. One day, a person with BPD may idealize you. The next, he or she can turn against you with venomous dislike.

People with borderline personality disorder often fluctuate between extremes in an incredibly short time. In their eyes, living is a black-and-white, all-or-nothing experience. Most of us have emotional "switches" equipped with dimmers. We can consciously respond to feelings and circumstances with heightened or decreased feeling. Individuals with BPD, however, seem to have only an "on-off" switch. Life is either fantastic or futile.

Currently, borderline personality disorder is the only psychological condition for which the DSM-IV specifically identifies self-injurious behaviors as a diagnostic criterion. Consequently, self-harmers may be incorrectly diagnosed with BPD. Qualified physicians and therapists can determine whether a person suffers from a full-blown borderline personality disorder or exhibits some, but not all, BPD tendencies.

Mandy, a therapist in San Diego, works with a self-harming woman, Sherri, who exhibits symptoms similar to those of a person suffering from borderline personality disorder. According to Mandy, Sherri is unstable, difficult to maintain relationship with, dramatic, and constantly creating drama. She often misreads communications and seems unable to see things from any point of view but her own (even though her perspective is often altered and nonfunctional).

This woman initially comes off as emotionally needy. Listening to her talk, it's easy to feel sorry for her. But on closer inspection, Sherri's view of reality is completely mired in "the world revolves around me and my issues" narcissism. Tragically, this narcissism stems from feelings of complete emptiness and a desperate need to develop some sense of self.

Mandy does not diagnose Sherri with BPD, but she says understanding some of this woman's behaviors in light of borderline personality disorder traits does help in therapy and treatment. It gives what Mandy describes as a framework for their shared journey toward recovery. Rather than viewing Sherri's choices strictly as selfish cries for attention, Mandy can see a broader picture of a deeply wounded woman searching for fulfillment and a strong personal identity.

There is no doubt that mood disorders affect, precipitate, or perpetuate many self-injurious behaviors. But officially classifying an individual as depressed, anxious, obsessive, or borderline may not be as important as recognizing how symptoms associated with one or more of these conditions influence the specific self-harmer you know. Rather than quick categorizations, careful observation and patient attention, coupled with consistent skilled medical treatment, will best help alleviate imbalances that accompany self-inflicted violence.

SHORTENED TIME HORIZON

Doctors Heather A. Berlin and Edmund T. Rolls conducted a protracted and intensive study of self-harming individuals, testing their impulsivity and emotionality. Results indicated that many self-injurers do or say things too quickly (without consideration), make rash decisions, and wish they could stop themselves from doing so.

Self-wounders like those in this study often suffer from what Rex Cowdry, former acting deputy director of the National Institute of Mental Health, describes as a shortened time horizon. A self-harmer's ability to think things through, problem solve, and see alternatives to instinctual reactions is sometimes significantly restricted.

Instead of delaying action prompted by urgent and intense feelings, many self-injurers act rashly, assuming their agitated emotional state will not end unless they wound themselves. On a virtual autopilot, self-harmers often leave little or no time between the overwhelming desire to hurt themselves and the act of doing so.

In order to begin healing, many self-wounders need help expanding their time horizons, lengthening the moments between urge and action by analyzing their situation and emotions.

Counseling helps many self-injurers develop patience to explore new ideas and alternatives to self-inflicted violence. Through counseling, those who wound themselves can receive explicit and immediate feedback when processing emotions linked to a shortened time horizon (for instance, "I *had* to cut. And I had to do it quick; nothing was getting better" can be turned into, "I really wanted to cut. But I thought about what else I could do. I decided to take a walk with my dog, and when I came back, I didn't feel like I *had* to hurt myself. I could see other options.").

Fortunately, people can learn to expand their time horizons in the same way we all learn that a sensation of hunger does not mean we have to eat immediately. We may *feel* that we need to, but if we want to or must wait, the intense feeling will fade or pass with time.

DISORDERED EATING

Some people include anorexia nervosa, bulimia nervosa, and binge eating disorder (BED) in the self-injury category. Having personally battled eating issues during high school and college, as well as having talked with self-harmers who struggle with disordered eating, I agree completely.

Like self-inflicted violence, anorexia, bulimia, and BED provide a way for individuals to relieve or release tension, cope with deep internal pain, communicate to others their heartache and need, and control an uncontrollable world.

People who cut or burn often attempt to reduce their complicated, messy lives to the simple experience of flowing blood or burning flesh. In an undeniably similar manner, people who battle disordered eating try to distill their problems to one weight- or food-driven reality.

Sufferers of both clinical eating disorders and other forms of self-harm usually report severe disturbances in body image and often feel incapable of understanding, let alone maintaining, physical boundaries. Many experience their bodies as a detached object, an "it" rather than "me."

At the same time self-injurers feel alienated from their bodies, an equally extreme preoccupation with the body can also plague them. Simultaneously viewing the body as an adversary to be conquered, controlled, and castigated, they also tend to obsess about hiding their scars and/or perfecting their figures.

Self-injury seems particularly prevalent among those with bulimic tendencies. In fact, Dr. Samuel Johnson, the eighteenth-century writer, scholar, and author of the first great English language dictionary, battled both of these conditions. From his journals, we learn that despite great achievements in literature and linguistics, Dr. Johnson led a "psychologically tortured existence marked by bouts of agitation, suicidal melancholy, and unremitting self-criticism."[8]

Unlike other forms of self-injury, anorexia and bulimia nervosa (in the form of exercising to purge) often start as a strategy to eat or exercise healthfully. For some, however, particularly those with unaddressed emotional or spiritual pain, food and workouts take on a life-destroying force of their own. Pleasure in healthy eating and exercise gives way to frenzied, guilt-driven despair. Compulsive behaviors continually progress to deeper degrees of self-destruction. Cutting, burning, bruising, or breaking may precipitate or follow this cycle of disordered eating.

We all know that our world presents extremely distorted messages about the body, food, and self. We use words like *sweetie* and *sugar* to describe people we love. We crave comfort food when we're sad or lonely, but we're constantly assaulted with images of men and women who look like they've never tasted an Oreo cookie. In light of this, it makes sense that so many people—especially young women—feel disconnected from or at odds with their bodies.

Through cutting, people try to deal with nebulous and endless emotional pain in a physical way. With an eating disorder, people attempt to manage and control psychological longings by converting them to physical sensations of hunger, fullness, or the temporary extinction of either. With food, blood, or both, people endeavor to indulge or deny their pain.

But the body *will* present its bill. Natural consequences of disordered eating may vary: Organs can give out, weight may refuse to come off or stay on, blood pressure might skyrocket or fall off a cliff. Author Marilee Strong says it best: "The body keeps score."[9]

For someone who struggles with both disordered eating and self-injury, confronting one of the issues individually may moderate tensions with the other. But simultaneously dealing with both, honestly and thoroughly, will provide the best results.

SMOTHERING RIGIDITY

Psychotherapist Jerilyn Robinson, who works at the S.A.F.E. Alternatives inpatient clinic in Illinois, reports that her clients are as likely to have smothering parents as neglectful or abusive ones. An enmeshed and/or dogmatic upbringing often precipitates and perpetuates self-wounding behavior.

Sixteen-year-old Cade's experience is one example of this. I grieve for this young man who used self-inflicted violence to escape—in the only way he felt he could—a suffocating home environment.

Cade's parents both grew up in emotionally impoverished families where verbal assaults were a part of everyday life and no one knew who was in charge. No one even cared. Determined not to repeat their parents' mistakes, Larry and Torrey established firm boundaries in their house and their children's lives.

The children went to bed at nine, no questions asked. Phone calls and Internet use were monitored carefully. Only rigidly supervised television or movies made it on to the family set. If family members wanted to listen to music in their rooms or the car, it had to be Christian praise. Larry and Torrey claimed they set down these rules out of love, but Cade didn't buy it. To him, everything (including religion) was used as a tool of overbearing control and oppression.

During adolescence, Cade started acting out in all kinds of ways. Furious at his parents' intrusive "love," he began to test the limits. Trying to establish himself as an individual, he dyed his hair black, pierced his nose and other places, and started cutting words like *hate* into his arms and legs.

At first Larry and Torrey tried to tighten the reins, forcing Cade to dye his hair back to a "normal" color and remove the rings from his body. But they couldn't stop the cutting. No matter how hard they tried to remove anything sharp from his grasp, Cade could always find some way to harm himself.

Though Larry and Torrey were well-meaning parents who wanted to protect their children from the freefall of neglect and abuse, families cannot rely on formulas to keep life safe and stable. Relationships — not rules — hold lives together. And in the absence of loving familial bonds, self-injurious rebellion and expression may crop up.

SOUL MURDER

According to studies performed by the S.A.F.E. Alternatives program and reported by the National Mental Health Association, close to 50 percent of self-injurers report that they were physically and/or sexually abused as a child.[10] Dr. Armando Favazza, pioneer self-harm researcher, believes that as many as 60 percent of self-wounders endured abuse at some point in their lives.[11]

For some who self-harm, discipline that came in the form of a black eye or inappropriate sexual touch, (mis)labeled as "loving attention," initiated their pattern of self-injury. For others, the equally pernicious but less obvious abuses of neglect or enmeshment just as easily sparked a life of self-harm.

Recurrent abuse, especially at the hands of a trusted loved one, is emotional annihilation of the highest order. It has been aptly, though heartbreakingly, described as "soul murder."

It's little wonder that victims of abuse struggle with self-injury in light of the fact that childhood trauma is very likely the biggest indicator of future mental illness, even more than being born with two schizophrenic parents.[12] In fact, the three million cases of childhood sexual abuse reported to authorities each year (which, due to the shameful and secretive nature of the issue, may be only a fraction of the actual occurrences) reflect a number *two times greater* than the annual new cases of cancer in the entire U.S. population. Imagine adding to the three million sexually abused children those unnumbered victims who experience physically violent, emotional, and/or verbal abuse. The idea is staggering—and horrifying. It seems safe to say that child abuse dwarfs—in both scope and magnitude—almost every mental-health concern related to self-harm.[13]

The long-term effects of childhood abuse that occurs frequently or over a long period of time are incredibly disastrous. In those cases where one family member violently assaults another, devastating ripples spread through the fabric of the entire family's existence. Dr. Mary Pipher, psychologist and author of *Reviving Ophelia: Saving the Selves of Adolescent Girls*, rightly asserts that sexual assault by a family member is a wound to the very soul of the family.

Totally dependent on their parents for basic needs and nurturing, children cannot bear to think their parents malevolent. Subsequently, victims of abuse usually assume responsibility—even if only subconsciously—for their parents' or other relatives' behavior.

Abused children fail to learn their own value. Never recognized as their own people with needs and desires, they are ever at the mercy of a more powerful person's twisted longings. Children of abuse therefore tend to shut down their emotions, bury their desires, and ignore their bodies' needs. Eventually, letting any feeling out seems so overwhelming that the victims refuse to acknowledge pain of any kind.

In his excellent book on sexual abuse, *The Wounded Heart*, Dr. Dan Allender acknowledges that years later, some people can't recognize they still hurt. Like that of a chronic, lingering toothache, their pain has become so familiar that it no longer interferes with daily tasks. The senses have been so dulled that to reintroduce the overwhelming shame of childhood abuse is unthinkable.[14]

In other instances, the past is a present reality that they relive with continual and agonizing trauma. Savagely attacking her body, which she felt had betrayed her during childhood, one woman expressed that she longed to cut her abuser out of her mind and his memory out of her body.

Because many victims of abuse view their bodies as helplessly broken, defiled, and filthy, the self-injurious tendency toward alienation from the body is a small, "logical" leap. Abused children—and the adults they grow up to be—also suffer under the burden of messages as implicit and psychologically devastating as the abuse itself: "You exist only to bring me pleasure [or provide an outlet for my anger]." "You deserve this." "If you had been a good little boy [or girl], this wouldn't have happened."

Some children feel sexually aroused during sexual abuse, which of course complicates matters even further. Victims like these feel complicit in the abuse because they experienced pleasure. Even if the stimulation they felt came involuntarily and perhaps against their earnest desire, they may spend the rest of their lives trying to punish the body that responded and the heart that felt special and sometimes enjoyed the abuser's attention (particularly if this was the only attention they received as children).

You can, with confidence, give these life-giving messages to every victim of abuse:

- What occurred is not your fault.
- There *is* a future hope, one stronger than your past.
- No matter what an abuser said, no matter what attention you craved, no matter what you did or felt before, during, and after the abuse, what occurred *is not* and *never will be* your fault.
- You are in *no way responsible* for the crimes committed against your body and heart.

If the self-injurer you know suffered or currently suffers in an abusive situation, please speak and reemphasize these messages. While victims may first receive these liberating truths with joy, the good news sometimes, tragically, loses its effectiveness. Transforming guilt to freedom is a long process.

Sadly, self-harmers sometimes replicate their original pain, acting out the very abuse they formerly suffered. Some do this as a means of self-punishment, others as a way to quell feelings of guilt. Still others cannot clearly pinpoint why they reenact their childhood wounds, but they express a powerful need to do so. They may recreate past wounds during flashbacks induced by post-traumatic stress disorder (PTSD). In order to understand this better, we'll look at some specific aspects of PTSD in the next section.

POST-TRAUMATIC STRESS DISORDER

After observing it in veterans of the Civil War and World War I, medical professionals initially called PTSD "war neurosis" or "shell shock." Doctors believed exploding shells on the battlefield literally rattled and shocked the brain. But though they studied the condition, they could rarely treat it effectively.

Clinicians now recognize PTSD as a disorder found not only in former soldiers but also in crime victims, refugees, abused people, and survivors of genocide campaigns. PTSD is *far more common* than most of us might imagine.

Those who endure protracted exposure to environmental stresses (famine, natural disaster, war) and those who witness horrific scenes often develop post-traumatic stress disorder. Children who lose parents or close loved ones early in life (whether through divorce or death) or suffer loss of special significance (for instance, the betrayal of a family member or abandonment by or alienation from friends or relatives) do as well.

Childhood trauma like this may result in PTSD or in symptoms associated with it. When a parent or child faces chronic illness (or any long-term physical condition, even those that eventually resolve), fear and loneliness, bitterness and resentment may overwhelm healthy family members. In an effort to deal with pain they cannot express without further wounding an already hurting family, these individuals may use self-inflicted violence to numb an aching heart.

A severely handicapped or seriously ill family member may absorb most of the energy and attention in a family. A child could sense that he or she needs to be strong for his or her parents, who (naturally so) need to attend more often to the sick person in their home.

And when death strikes a family, grief can sap parents, children, and siblings of the resources to love one another well. This void may precipitate a family member's self-injury.

Many victims of abuse also develop PTSD-like symptoms. Some battle full-blown post-traumatic stress disorder. Throughout the remainder of this section, I will discuss PTSD as a result of abuse as the case example. But while reading, keep in mind that the experience of unpredictability, instability, and fear felt by abuse victims can also mark the lives of individuals exposed to other forms of trauma, such as those just mentioned.

Victims of abuse face overwhelming horror and stress comparable to soldiers of war. The same long-term and inescapable anxiety, uncertainty, and vulnerability plague them. In fact, childhood victims of abuse may suffer from *more* trauma than combat veterans. Soldiers have been trained, equipped with weapons, and set within a company who fight with them, backing them up and often protecting them. Children living in abusive situations, however, usually have no way to defend themselves, though they often (and for good reason) fear for their lives. They exist in the perpetual and unpredictable fear both of being found out and never being found out. The shame of abuse—particularly sexual abuse—often keeps victims locked in silence and secrecy, as do the threats abusers frequently make (for example, "If you tell, I'll kill you [or someone you love or myself].") At the same time, imagining that the abuse will continue forever deadens victims' hope for the future.

Adults and children process emotions differently. Young people are neither physically nor psychologically equipped to confront trauma. Instead, with childish intensity, they mobilize primitive physiological and emotional defenses. Unless their trauma can be effectively processed, victims of childhood abuse never get beyond the stage of development at which abuse arrested them.

Encompassing years of psychological and biological research, Dr. Bessel van der Kolk's evidence indicates that both brain structure and chemistry, as well as other systems that help the body deal with stress, can be dramatically altered as a result of abuse. This proves particularly true if the trauma occurs before the child's central nervous system has fully developed. Neurologically immature, children simply *cannot* process the repeated and destructive overstimulation that accompanies abuse. As a result, the body fails to respond appropriately to physical and emotional cues.

Dr. Daniel Amen, the neuropsychiatrist with whom Dr. Henslin and I have worked, has helped pioneer the use of a form of brain imaging so advanced and illustrative that it has changed, and will continue to change, the face of mental-health care. It's called, for short, SPECT (single photon emission computed tomography). During a SPECT scan, three-dimensional "snapshots" of the brain (at rest and while concentrating) are formed after the SPECT machine takes more than ten thousand pictures of the brain's surface and interior.

On the most simplistic level, SPECT scanning allows clinicians to evaluate the areas of a person's brain that are working well, those that are not working hard enough, and those that are overworking. After identifying the distressed parts of a person's brain, a SPECT scan then enables clinicians to determine what kinds of treatment, based on all the physiological clues, will be most efficacious.

Now, I realize some of you may be thinking, *What does all this have to do with me and the self-injurer I care about? Does someone have to undergo a SPECT scan to get better?*

No. There are many ways that self-harmers can find help and healing. Brain imaging is one of them, but certainly not the only one. If a SPECT scan, or a similar treatment, is not available to the self-injurer you care about, do not despair.

We've simply chosen to include information about SPECT scanning in this chapter and the next for two reasons. First, seeing clear evidence of physical issues that influence a person's struggle with self-inflicted violence reminds us that we should help the people we love choose clinicians and forms of therapy wisely. Effectively combating self-harm takes more than simplistic answers or trial-and-error medical "guinea pigging."

Second, and perhaps more important, looking at even one brain scan can help loved ones better comprehend the physiological battle that some self-wounders face. Things like SPECT imaging reveal the complex nature of the human brain, which helps us understand a deeper level to self-injury than meets the eye. To help us truly visualize this, Dr. Amen has agreed to let us look at two SPECT scans.

The second scan, that of an individual prone to self-injurious behaviors, displays what Dr. Amen refers to as a "diamond-plus" pattern. Having studied for nearly two decades the SPECT images of people exposed to trauma, Dr. Amen informed me that when "we get traumatized the emotional part of the brain fires up or becomes inflamed. On scans, [this appears as a] diamond pattern, with increased activity in [several significant areas of] the brain."

But before we get there, let's look at the scan of a healthy brain. In order to help us more clearly contrast the first and second scans, we have marked important areas of the brain and explained their functions.

Normal SPECT Scan

Used by permission, courtesy of the Amen Clinic

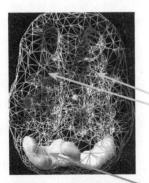

healthy brain, outside view

Prefrontal Cortex

Controls attention, concentration, forethought, judgment, and impulse control. This is the part of the brain that helps people say no to harmful urges (such as those to self-injure). Within the PFC is the orbital frontal cortex, which helps with the self-regulation of feelings and conscience.

Temporal Lobes

Help a healthy person read social cues and facial expressions, retrieve language, facilitate long-term memory, and maintain emotional stability.

Basal Ganglia

These portions of the brain act—with the cingulate—as "gear shifters," helping people transition from one thought pattern to another. In a healthy brain, the basal ganglia, which also control the level of anxiety throughout the body, are "cool" (in this scan hardly visible). In the brains of self-injurious people, however, the basal ganglia are often significantly larger, inflamed, and "hot."

Cerebellum

The most active portion of healthy brains, the cerebellum functions as the center for motor control. It also connects to the prefrontal cortex and plays an important role in executive functioning and cognitive integration.

healthy brain, inside view

Normal SPECT Scan
Used by permission, courtesy of the Amen Clinic

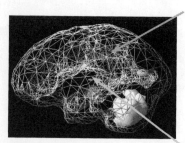

healthy brain, inside profile view

Cingulate

Because the cingulate shown here is "cool," this person would be able to shift away from negative thoughts about self and the world around him or her. He or she would be able to choose to call for support or encouragement. This person would be able to take steps of self-care.

Deep Limbic System

A healthy limbic system keeps the body's emotional tone balanced, modulates motivation, and maintains appetite, sleep, and libido cycles. It also aids in processing and storing emotionally charged memories.

As you can see, a healthy brain shows full, even, symmetrical activity throughout the prefrontal cortex. The cerebellum (which manages motor control and plays a key role in cognitive functions such as attention and the processing of language and temporary sensory stimuli) is the most active portion of healthy brains.

And according to the scan of a healthy brain, normal activity levels in the emotional and cognitive centers of the brain (including the cingulate, basal ganglia, and temporal lobes), as well as in the portion of the brain that controls mood, sleep, appetite, and sexual cycles (the deep limbic system), are consistent and, as Dr. Amen terms it, "cool."

When areas of the brain get "hot" (activity is markedly intensified on the scan), a person experiences disturbances in physical and mental health. For instance, while a healthy cingulate and basal ganglia allow a person to be, as Dr. Amen describes, "flexible, adaptable, and open to change as needed," overactivity in either of these sections of the brain can lead to anxiety (including panic attacks), rigid and contentious thinking and conduct, and even addictive behavior.[15]

We can see all of this in the following brain scan, the "hot" brain of a self-harmer, which presents itself in a diamond pattern. Seriously heightened levels of activity in the areas of the brain that control emotion, cognition, and healthy physical functioning are evident, which result in obsession, depression, and an inability to move forward after trauma and anxiety.

Abnormal SPECT Scan

Used by permission, courtesy of the Amen Clinic

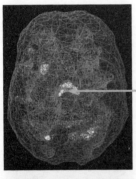

A "hot" limbic system like this indicates deep depression. This person reported difficulty in connecting with other people and finding supportive relationships, which is often characteristic of traumatized or depressed individuals with overactive deep limbic systems.

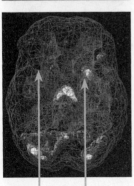

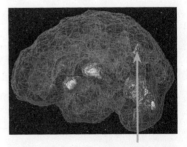

The anterior cingulate is also working overtime, making it difficult to let go of obsessive thoughts and compulsive behaviors.

These basal ganglia are significantly overactive, which intensifies this person's experience of anxiety and pain.

distressed brain, inside view

Abnormal SPECT Scan
Used by permission, courtesy of the Amen Clinic

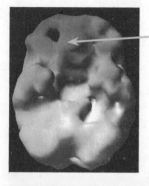

Here we see decreased perfusion in the prefrontal cortex. This results in impulsiveness and a lack of self-awareness. Under stress, this person would struggle to see the potential outcome of self-destructive actions.

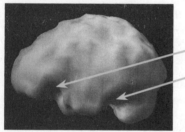

An observable injury in the temporal lobes helps explain this person's inability to control moods in a healthy manner.

distressed brain, outside view

Dr. Amen claims that, like the self-wounder whose scan we just viewed, those who self-injure almost always deal with other psychiatric issues concurrently. He has seen PTSD and depression most commonly connected with self-inflicted violence.

The symptoms of PTSD include invasive and recurrent memories, dreams, and nightmares connected with the distressing events; dissociative flashbacks (which will be discussed briefly in the next section); feelings of isolation and alienation; and emotional numbing and/or hypervigilance. Sufferers often find it difficult to sleep, concentrate, set personal boundaries, form trusting relationships, and either express or control anger. Constant foreboding robs the present of pleasure and the future of hope.

As the abused person attempts to adapt to chronic anxiety and over-stimulation, his or her stress-response system can eventually become underresponsive to stress signals. This explains why many sufferers of PTSD report persistent and debilitating numbness.

Victims of abuse often produce significantly higher levels of cortisol, a hormone released by the adrenal gland during "fight or flight" situations. Too much cortisol can damage brain cells connected with learning and memory, as well as suppress the immune system. Internalizing emotional trauma and converting it to physiological symptoms (a process known as somatization) can lead to headaches, digestive problems, and other physical pains.

A variety of factors may increase a victim's propensity to PTSD. The more terrified and helpless a person feels, the more closely connected he or she feels to the perpetrator, the deeper the degree of shame and guilt, and the lack of support (including rejection or blaming) the person receives, the greater the risk he or she will develop PTSD.

Swiss psychologist Alice Miller poignantly provides a final word for the way devastating childhood experiences mark people forever. She writes, "The truth about childhood is stored up in our body and lives in the depth of our soul. Our intellect can be deceived, our feelings can be numbed and manipulated, our perception shamed and confused, our bodies tricked with medication. But our soul never forgets."[16]

DISSOCIATION

Many self-injurers experience a unique physical sensation called dissociation. This complex physiological response to trauma can be present during flashbacks or as a means of self-protection during especially stressful situations.

Every one of us understands dissociation, though the majority of us wouldn't know to call our experiences by their proper medical name. Have you ever driven past your freeway exit while "lost" in another thought? Have you ever "tuned out" while someone talked your ear off?

Do you sometimes forget the last sentence you read or start forming a grocery list in the midst of praying for a sick friend?

Self-injurers experience dissociations like these, but they can also suffer from dissociative states of a more severe degree. Looking at the continuum of dissociation, accidentally overshooting your destination would be a mild form. At the extreme end of the continuum, we would find mental disintegration that affects memory, state of consciousness, and physical feeling.

On this level, dissociation serves as a psychological defense mechanism against traumatic memories or situations that a person cannot physically or emotionally integrate. An "ingenious bit of mental gymnastics,"[17] dissociation allows individuals to depersonalize an experience, anesthetize themselves to pain, and get "outside" themselves.

While victims may not be able to physically remove themselves from danger or severe emotional pain, through dissociation, they can temporarily "space out," observing their experiences or actions as a dispassionate onlooker. Repeated dissociation like this, however, can fragment the psyche, ultimately disconnecting a person from his or her own reality.

Katie, the self-injurious heroine of Steven Levenkron's novel *The Luckiest Girl in the World*, suffers from recurrent dissociation. Her therapist describes the condition well:

> So here's what happens to you when you "space out." You experience an emotion that you can't handle—either because it's too strong and painful, or because you've been taught it's something you're not allowed to feel, or some combination of those factors. . . . Because the response that is triggered is too powerful for you, you enter what we call a dissociated state. Which is a fancy way of saying your mind goes blank until the threatening feeling dissipates. It's as if you'd fainted but you're still conscious.[18]

Amazingly, self-injury can act as a "toggle switch" between dissociative states. Self-inflicted violence can provide a powerful and expulsive experience that ends the mental disintegration of a dissociative assault, *or* it can induce dissociation for people who want to "get outside themselves."

Since self-injury quite effectively focuses a person's attention on the physical body, it often increases self-awareness. In doing so, it can halt a person's descent into dissociation. On the other hand, people who suffer from abuse can use dissociation to space out during acts of violence perpetrated against them. People who fear the act of self-injury can also teach themselves to space out before and while hurting themselves, altering their consciousness and blurring their sensation of physical stimuli. This is somewhat akin to the often-successful use of hypnosis to blunt or anesthetize the pain of medical procedures.

Serious problems arise for self-harmers who dissociate before or during their self-injurious acts. In *Cutting*, Steven Levenkron relates the story of a victim of heinous, incestuous abuse who frequently "lost time." She would "come to" hours later, often bleeding and remembering nothing about her wounds. In this kind of trance, she felt no physical pain while hurting herself. But she also could have injured herself so severely that she severed an artery and bled to death. Clearly, a self-injurer's dissociation must be confronted.

If a self-harmer has learned to dissociate, the behavior can be unlearned, but it does require significant effort. The unconscious use of dissociation to induce an altered state of being proves a more difficult act to treat. A person suffering in this way will need both consistent and long-term medical and therapeutic intervention to recover.

AN ESCAPE OR AN EXIT?

In the "Self Injury Fact Sheet" she published online, Deb Martinson, chair of the American Self-Harm Information Clearinghouse, explains that "self-injury is VERY RARELY a failed suicide attempt. People who inflict physical harm on themselves are often doing it in an attempt to maintain psychological integrity—it's a way to keep from killing themselves."[19] Rather than an exit strategy, self-inflicted violence serves as a "life preserver" for people drowning in emotional pain. In the words of one self-harmer, she is slowly "dying to survive."

Dr. Tracy Alderman confirms: "As is commonly said, [suicide] is a permanent solution to a temporary problem. . . . In contrast, self-inflicted violence is used to cope [or] adapt to severe psychological discomfort. You hurt yourself so you can feel better. This goal of feeling better is in direct contrast with suicide's goal of not feeling at all."[20]

Substance abuse and eating disorders can be lethal at extreme levels. But we rarely suspect bulimics or alcoholics of being suicidal. Instead, we see them as facing a difficult problem, but one that can be treated and eventually overcome. The same is true of those who self-injure.

As we mentioned in the last chapter, people who wound themselves may battle suicidal thoughts. In fact, suicidal ideation accompanies many cases of self-inflicted violence. Usually, however, self-injurers stop short of ending their lives. Instead, by hurting themselves, they find a temporary escape. Ironically, some self-wounders use cutting or burning to get rid of suicidal thoughts.

Still, as *Registered Nurse* magazine reports, although "individuals who physically harm themselves usually aren't suicidal . . . they're 18 times more likely than the general population to die at their own hand by causing more harm than they intended."[21]

Whether struggling with suicidal impulses or not, self-harmers will benefit from understanding that their self-injurious behaviors can lead to accidental death. Where suicidal ideation is present, a combination of therapy and medication (professional help is especially important in such cases) will help address the feelings and experiences that perpetuate thoughts of suicide.

A FINAL NOTE

Through this chapter we've seen that a number of physiological and psychological conditions can influence a person's battle with self-harm.

People who wound themselves may suffer from the trauma of past abuse. They may feel crippled by depression or an eating disorder. They may live in or have grown up in a stifling environment.

But none of these is cause for hopelessness. Of course, any of us would feel sorrow after discovering that someone we care about faces not only self-injurious tendencies but also deep-seated accompanying issues. Equipped with information and committed to recovery, however, self-injurers can experience healing in *everything* that plagues them.

4 IS IT ALL IN THEIR HEAD?
THE UNDENIABLE INFLUENCE OF PHYSIOLOGY IN SELF-INJURY

We previously observed that for some people, cutting feels like an organic *need* rather than a conscious choice. Depression or anxiety, the trauma of past abuse, or simply vulnerable chemistry may lead to and then perpetuate self-injurious behaviors. This happened to a dear friend of mine, a brilliant, creative, and passionate woman. Eileen offered to let us inside her world for a brief time. Here is her story:

> The door flung open as Janice threw herself into the hall. She glanced at my forearm and blanched. Looking me squarely in the eye, with fierce determination in her voice, Janice told me, "You need a chiliburger."
>
> At 10:30 a.m., the last thing I thought I needed was a hamburger. And it seemed rather strange that instead of asking me why I had been repeatedly slashing my hand and wrist with a pin, Janice wanted to take me to Tommy's (a glorified fast-food joint half an hour from our college).
>
> But in the thirty minutes between the business department classroom at my university and the greasy goodness that a chiliburger offered, I calmed down. I could almost laugh at the crazy way I'd attacked myself. But not quite.
>
> The whole thing scared me. I had no idea why it made

perfect sense to start cutting my forearm, let alone do it over and over again. But I did know that it felt good. Well, maybe not *good*, but at least better.

Greg had broken up with me two weeks before my sophomore-year finals. He was the first and only real boyfriend I'd had, and our split seemed to disrupt my entire existence. I couldn't concentrate on the tests looming ahead, the projects and papers that had to be finished in fourteen days or less. All I could feel was this raging, hurting, threatening swell inside me. I was sure it would overtake me any minute. My mind spun constantly, and my body felt perpetually tense and attacked. It all seemed too much.

So in the middle of Dr. Mason's lecture on Latin-American trade practices, I unceremoniously left the room and used the pin I found while rummaging in my purse to cut my arm, to make it bleed. That's when Janice found me.

Though she seemed calm enough to me that day, she later confided that she totally flipped out inside. Now I understand why. What if I had followed Janice out of class and watched her rip into the skin on her forearm? I'd have freaked out too. But back then, on the other side of the equation, I felt strangely calm and rational.

Janice's "take me to Tommy's" tactic worked well. It distracted me from the tide of fear, pain, and anger inside me. And the intensity of finals helped push the anguish of Greg and the breakup out of my mind.

But I remembered—vividly—what it felt like to slice my own skin. I recalled the way each rivulet of blood looked as it slowly oozed from the shallow cuts on my hand. I remembered most of all that it *worked*. It soothed me. It stanched the flow of my internal wounds.

Cutting never became what I'd call a habit, but it definitely followed me around after that first incident. It became an option, a last-ditch effort when fierce mental-emotional assaults terrorized me.

I cut off and on during the lonely years of my first marriage when my husband, Jeff, made it clear that all that mattered was his life and whether I would support him.

Jeff berated me constantly. When I told him I might want to explore singing and composing, he actually laughed in my face. He also told me I didn't need a car because nothing I wanted to do was that important. Furthermore, we didn't need to be spending money—which was already tight—on "frivolous things" like transportation for me.

When our problems increased, Jeff stopped communicating with me. He adamantly refused to discuss uncomfortable emotions or difficult situations. He also forbade me from talking about anything negative with my friends or family. Not only was I physically isolated, thousands of miles from the people who knew and loved me most, I was forcibly emotionally distanced from anyone who might have supported me in the loveless void of my marriage.

I felt trapped and angry and so depressed. I knew I couldn't leave Jeff—in my religion divorce was *not* an option. And it would absolutely kill my parents. But I grew increasingly desperate. I had no one. At some point, I realized that a pit so deep and dark had swallowed me that I couldn't get out on my own.

It would have been nice if someone had reached out to me then. But even the church seemed to turn its back on me. People kept telling me to "have more faith" or "look at the good things in your life." And I wanted to. I didn't want to be depressed. I tried to jump out of the pit. I tried so hard. But I kept falling deeper and deeper into gloomy emptiness. I would cut now and then, but even that stopped helping.

The weekend my older brother got married, Jeff announced that he didn't love me anymore. But it didn't matter, he assured me. Our marriage was "working" for him, so we shouldn't bother changing anything.

As you can imagine, I felt totally crushed. I not only cut but injuriously exercised and wounded myself by binging on or restricting my food. Sure, I wanted to be so beautiful Jeff would desire me, but I didn't care as much about losing weight as I did controlling what seemed horribly unmanageable.

A short while later, Jeff got in a car accident that sent him to the hospital for a week. While there, he met and fell in love with Amy. My marriage was over. And somewhat surprisingly, I got on with life pretty well.

I met and started dating a man who told me how crazy Jeff was to let me slip away. Keith appreciated my artistic side and seemed to value and understand me in a way Jeff never had. I actually hoped for something better than I had experienced with Jeff. But things with Keith weren't perfect either.

He couldn't comprehend why I grieved the end of my marriage. I was with him now; I should be happy . . . or so he thought. Keith dealt with life by turning off any emotional spigot that let hurt or anger escape. While Jeff had stormed and raged, Keith iced with stony silence anything that threatened his carefully, calmly constructed inner world.

Still, things with Keith were pretty good until he invited me camping. He thought experiencing the "great outdoors" together would move our relationship to the next level.

He didn't plan for the extreme motion sickness our three-hour drive through twisty mountain passes would give me. He didn't know that I'd be menstruating and crazy with emotion. And he had no idea that the campground he loved would look filthy to me. Keith and I broke up before we got home.

Naturally (or so I considered it to be), I went home and cut myself. But this time I sliced lower and harder than I ever had before. I'm still not sure if I wanted to die or not. But I definitely could have taken my own life if Keith hadn't called in the middle of my self-attack. Don't ask me why, but I told Keith what I had done. He took me to the hospital, and I finally began to confront the problems that plagued me.

As the doctors evaluated me, they helped me see that my mental-physical health and the circumstances of my life influenced one another in seriously destructive ways.

I used cutting to make the torrential pain inside me visible, tangible. I wanted to know—and wanted other people to know—that my hurt was *real*. Someone might tell me I had no reason to be sad or anxious, but they couldn't argue with bleeding wounds. Through my self-inflicted injuries, I screamed, "See! I'm wounded. And this is how much."

I couldn't just "snap myself" out of the depression or anxiety that had haunted me for years just because I wanted to or because people told me I should. I also had the right to, and *needed*, to grieve the broken dreams that contributed to my physical issues.

The psychiatrist I started seeing regularly prescribed new medications for me. Some worked; some didn't. A couple of them made me want to self-injure more (obviously those weren't the right drugs for me); others cut me off from my emotions and made me feel dead inside (which was the last thing I wanted to experience).

Even though trying a bunch of different meds frustrated me a bit, getting out of that dark, depressed pit made everything worth it. After some intense soul searching and finally taking the right medication, I started to realize that I didn't have to create a reason to be depressed. What I mean by that is that people kept asking why I felt so badly, but I didn't even know. I couldn't identify exactly why; I was just *depressed*. Cutting gave me something to point to. It helped me explain, reveal, and justify my depression.

A big part of my recovery was coming to terms with the fact that my body was needy. I couldn't just "stop cutting" or "stop feeling sad." I couldn't turn off despair and flip the switch to joy. And ironically, that has been one of the most freeing things in my life and one of the greatest motivations on the path to recovery.

BOTH/AND

Was Eileen's major problem physical or circumstantial? Would she have cut if she didn't struggle with depression? Would she have battled self-injury if her marriage hadn't been so devoid of love and understanding? Clearly, Eileen benefited from taking medication for depression and anxiety. What does the efficacy of psychotropic drugs in Eileen's experience reveal about the connection between emotions and the body?

Over the next few pages, we're going to explore some vitally important material. You may never have imagined that learning about the brain and its biochemistry could enable you to better comprehend and help the self-wounders in your life. Believe me, it can; *it will*. To understand the kind of self-inflicted violence with which some people (like Eileen) struggle, it's absolutely essential that we investigate the intimate connections between physical and mental health.

Hippocrates taught the earliest physicians that sickness and well-being result from a complex interaction between the body, the environment, and the soul (including, but not limited to, the mind). At roughly the same time, Chinese healers observed that people almost always became physically ill after particularly painful emotional experiences.

This holistic, integrated view of health changed drastically in the seventeenth century when mathematician and philosopher René Descartes posited that the mind and body were separate entities. According to Descartes, the body acted as a machine, obeying the same mathematical and physical laws that governed the universe, while the mind—dimensionless and spiritual—existed outside the material world.

Scientists during the Age of Reason grabbed hold of this hypothesis, which became known as the mind-body split. Wanting to exclude theology and what we would call psychology from the study of the physical body, practitioners seized the paradox of a disconnected mind and soul and then built much of modern medicine on that foundation.

But self-injurers are "living proof that when the body is ravaged, the soul cries out. And when the soul is trampled upon, the body bleeds."[1]

Many professionals, foremost among them psychologists who daily observe the interplay between physical and mental health, now seek to reverse the historical attempt to separate the mind, body, and soul. Fortunately, holistic care of individuals has received greater attention and practice over the last couple of decades.

Processing the following information will help you understand not only self-harmers but also those in your life who battle depression, anxiety, or any number of conditions. Despite the opinions we have formed in the past, let's explore the mind-body-soul connection with an open mind and heart.

THE POWER OF TOUCH

Did you know that both the skin and the brain grow from the same embryonic cell layer, the ectoderm? From a person's earliest days, the skin provides a primary way to experience the world. Babies sleep peacefully or coo when cuddled and nurtured; they cry when cold. They throw fits when they want to be held.

As we grow and mature, the skin not only receives continuous sensory input from the world around us, but it also becomes a significant organ of communication. We express and experience pleasure and pain, tenderness and hostility with our skin.

Through the skin, signals enter the brain, traveling quickly to the thalamus, a section of the brain that attempts to make sense of incoming physical messages.

Instantly sent from the thalamus, pleasant or painful signals arrive in both the prefrontal cortex (PFC) and the deep limbic system (DLS). As way of a minireview, the PFC is where conscious thinking and analysis take place, and the DLS governs emotions and bodily functions. "When this happens, your thinking brain and your emotional brain have a dialogue, in which they 'compare notes' on the . . . signal."[2]

During this dialogue, your cortex and limbic system decide how to react. In the case of pain, if the signals aren't very serious, your brain's neurotransmitter system pumps out calming brain chemicals, causing the muscles to relax and blood vessels, which have been constricted by the threat of danger, to expand.

During a state of emergency, however, pain signals travel to a part of the limbic system called the amygdala. This tiny, almond-shaped sector at the base of the brain, which works like an elaborate alarm system, translates physical threats into altered facial expressions, physical tension, and chemical changes in the brain, all of which help the body prepare for danger.

In addition, according to University of Michigan and Columbia University researchers who explored the effectiveness of placebos in relieving anticipated pain, "Findings acknowledge that pain is a psychologically constructed experience. . . . The pain we feel seems to be a product of the sensory information we encounter and the unique ways in which we process these sensations."[3]

Apparently, whether the body feels relief or greater stress after receiving a threatening signal can be controlled by the particular way an individual's brain manages sensory input.

If you recall, I mentioned earlier that self-injury does not always hurt. And as we've heard from people who have battled self-harm, cutting or burning often tends to produce feelings of calm and reprieve.

This can be explained by the following: After engaging in self-inflicted violence, most self-injurers' brains solicit the involvement of the endogenous opioid system, which regulates pain perception and levels of the body's natural pain-relieving chemicals—endorphins, dynorphins, and enkephalins (collectively known as opiates).

Endorphins, dynorphins, and enkephalins help the body feel pleasure and control the sensation of pain. Dr. Daniel Amen told me that opiates "make us feel happy, content, normal."

Drugs such as heroin, opium, and morphine work by imitating the action of the body's inborn opiates. In fact, scientists actually formed the term *endorphin* by combining the words *morphine* and *endogenous* (naturally occurring in the body). But the body's instinctive painkillers, its morphinelike opioids, are stronger — *eight to ten times stronger* — than morphine.

Don't miss this startling fact: When opiates are released through self-wounding, it's as if self-harmers have been given eight to ten doses of one of the most powerful pain-numbing drugs known to man.

Isn't that amazing? At the same time, isn't that tragic? Since Dr. Amen informed me that natural opiates "tend to be low in people who are cutters, and the act of cutting raises opiates," it seems completely, though cruelly, logical that self-injurers would *crave* the release of these chemicals that make them feel happy, content, and normal.

Since scientists can clinically observe increased levels of endorphins in the body after self-inflicted violence, it also makes sense that self-harmers feel physical and emotional relief after hurting themselves. Some, anticipating this release, even experience tingling and excited sensations before and/or during self-wounding acts. Others actually feel exhilarated after inflicting violence on themselves.

Because of these powerful physical forces, using self-injury to combat pain could seem initially reasonable to people who ache for relief. And it certainly proves effective in providing release, at least at first. But just as the body quickly builds up a tolerance for euphoria-inducing drugs like morphine, heroin, and opium, the brain can also become accustomed to, and then numbed to, the effects of natural opiate release.

As early as 1983, British scientists reported "markedly higher" levels of enkephalins (an opiate similar to the better-known endorphins) in self-injurers who cut recently. Those who had not self-harmed in two months or more exhibited decreased enkephalin levels.[4] Pleasure-inducing chemicals last for only a short while. This explains why many self-harmers express that, over time, they need to cut more often and more severely to produce the same effects they readily felt when first self-wounding.

After years of study, Dr. Bessel van der Kolk concludes that the self-harmer's body may develop a conditioned response to highly charged physical-emotional experiences. While self-injury may have first produced a heightened level of opiates, it ultimately causes numbing.

When habitual self-harmers attempt to stop cutting or burning, they may actually experience opiate withdrawal similar to what recovering heroin addicts undergo. Aggressive behaviors, hyperactivity, and excessive anxiety may threaten to overwhelm them. Many give in and start an even more vicious cycle of self-inflicted violence.

During an interview with Dr. Amen, I learned that some medical professionals believe people can be born with a greater number of opiate receptors in the prefrontal cortex. A self-injurer in this situation may be at greater risk for dependence on the naturally occurring morphinelike chemicals produced in the brain.

It's essential to recognize that the opioid system plays a significant role in self-inflicted violence. A person's unique genetic makeup also acts in significant ways. For some, self-injury seems to stem from what we might call "vulnerable" chemistry.

"VULNERABLE" CHEMISTRY

Some people live through unbearably awful childhood or adolescent experiences but grow up to lead emotionally stable lives. On the flip side, others come from relatively "normal" and happy homes but still struggle with debilitating psychological difficulties.

This makes it clear that a person's innate temperament and physical makeup help determine how he or she deals with mental anguish and explains why one member of a family — even one treated as equitably and lovingly as possible — becomes a self-injurer while another does not.

In addition to the biochemical changes similar to substance addiction that we just investigated, other natural physical conditions unique to each person may spark and perpetuate patterns of self-inflicted violence. Self-harm can be linked to decreased serotonin activity, temporal lobe dysfunction, excessive levels of the neurotransmitter dopamine, and poor executive functioning. Too much dopamine in the brain makes clear and rational thinking more difficult. Decreased serotonin levels often cause depression, and temporal lobe malfunctioning leads to a host of issues, including learning difficulties and problems with memory, language retrieval, and even the development of social skills. All of these situations can contribute to an individual's self-injurious behavior.

Additionally, the prefrontal cortex (which makes most of a person's "executive decisions") continues to develop after birth and even across an individual's lifespan. We can easily observe—for instance, in comparing preschoolers with college students—that a conscious ability to control thoughts, actions, and emotions grows over time. In addition, we can see that the younger people are, the more their knowledge about what *should* be done surpasses their ability to actually follow through with that intelligence.

Being able to act in concert with one's knowledge comprises a significant part of the brain's executive functioning. But the development of this particular aspect of the prefrontal cortex's work follows what Dr. Philip David Zelazo calls an "extremely protracted development course that extends well into adolescence and probably into early adulthood."[5]

If the maturity of executive functioning in the brain does not keep to this "normal" track because of genetic factors—or if it is delayed or halted due to severe trauma such as abuse—aggressive mood swings, attention problems, suicidal ideation, obsessive preoccupation, impulsive risk taking, and compulsive behaviors may result. The self-wounder with poor executive functioning could exhibit one or all of these problems.[6]

For many self-harmers, mental disorders (such as anxiety, depression, and OCD) are chemically present in varying hereditary degrees.

These genetic predispositions toward imbalance range from relatively minimal to life-debilitating. And other brain dysfunctions can significantly increase a person's likelihood of self-injury. This happened to one bright, talented, and tortured self-harmer whose story I came across in Marilee Strong's book *A Bright Red Scream*. We'll call this young woman, an aspiring filmmaker and screenwriter, Carissa.

For as long as Carissa could remember, it felt impossible to silence the "inner critics" that controlled her mind. Sometimes the noise would just get too loud and awful. Cutting seemed the only escape, but since it lasted for only a short time, Carissa found she had to wound herself over and over again with increasing severity.

After several failed attempts at recovery, Carissa submitted herself to a brain scan. By studying the scan, her doctors found two small cysts on her brain, which they believed caused seizures that translated into the noise in Carissa's mind.

Placed on the antiepileptic medicine Tegretol (which proved effective for other self-injurers in a National Institute of Mental Health study), Carissa experienced relief from the self-destructive messages in her head. Her self-inflicted violence also decreased significantly.

Carissa also worked with a therapist and addressed other potential genetic connections (for instance, although Carissa had not been diagnosed as bipolar herself, both her mother and grandmother battled the condition). Through a combination of physical and psychotherapeutic treatment, Carissa found that she did not need to use cutting in an attempt to control her life, the noise in her mind, or her reaction to it.[7]

I wanted to share Carissa's story with you because we can best help self-harmers by exploring with them *all* the physical and genetic possibilities that may contribute to their self-injury. A ravaged body can lead to an anguished mind and soul. But sometimes the only way we can learn about this is with the help of licensed professionals. It's not intuitive stuff. I would never have known to recommend an antiseizure medication for Carissa.

In order to understand and help some of the self-wounders in our lives, it will benefit many of us to learn even more about the brain's role in self-inflicted violence. Let me allow Dr. Henslin, as a professional who can explain complex things in simple and practical ways, take us through the most important lesson in biochemistry we may ever have.

──────────── IN MY EXPERIENCE ────────────

By Dr. Earl Henslin

As Beth walked into my office and nervously sank into the corner of the couch (which she very clearly wanted to hide in), I noticed the white bandages that covered her right arm from wrist to elbow.

After treating the thirty-five plus cuts on Beth's arm, some deep enough to require stitches, Beth's family physician referred her to me. This frenzy of cutting was not Beth's first excursion into the confused world where people find relief through inflicting pain on their own bodies. Beth's first attempt to physically cope with pain in her soul occurred at the age of twelve, after being sexually abused by her grandfather.

A bewildering and devastating mixture of terror, pleasure, and shame flooded Beth's mind and heart during and after the experience with her grandfather. It's difficult for most of us to understand how someone could feel pleasure in sexual abuse. But even if someone like Beth wants—with all of her heart and mind—to avoid sexual stimulation while being mistreated, the body often responds anyway. Abusive sexual touch is not always violent or forceful. People like Beth sometimes experience enjoyable sensations, even orgasm, despite the horrific reality of their situation.

Over the years, Beth's body and soul forged a virtually unbreakable link between pain and pleasure. The guilt and shame was so strong, the fear that she had caused her grandfather to do this was so overwhelming, that Beth could find secret release only by slicing the inside of her upper thigh with a razor blade. Cutting temporarily overrode the conflicted memories connected with her grandfather's abuse.

Beth became sexually promiscuous at an early age, and by twenty she could list dozens of different partners. Her latest bout of compulsive cutting resulted when an affair with a man in her church who was fifteen years older than her and married with two small children ended.

I administered on Beth the Amen Brain Subsystems Checklist[8] (created, of course, by Dr. Amen), a test that measures the functioning of five different brain systems in any person. This checklist often provides me with initial insight into how a person's brain chemistry contributes to his or her present problems.

The Amen Brain Subsystems Checklist asks patients like Beth to rate one hundred questions regarding their behavior and thought patterns using a six-point scale, with zero meaning "never," four meaning "very frequently," and "NA" meaning "not applicable/not known." To provide a more complete picture, supervising clinicians also recommend that another person who knows the patient well complete the checklist at the same time. Because others can observe things the patient may not be able to see, having someone close to the patient can give me or another professional a more complete picture of his or her behavior. For each of the five subsystems the checklist evaluates, a person responds to multiple descriptive statements (for example, "I have a tendency to get locked in a course of action, whether or not it is good," "I live in excessive fear of being judged or scrutinized by others," and "I often misinterpret comments as negative when they are not"), which helps doctors like me evaluate how well certain parts of the brain are working.

Answering "very frequently" to one question does not suggest a person needs medical treatment. Instead, through a wide variety of queries on the checklist (and using what I know about a patient's history and personality through therapy or observation), I try to put together as complete a picture as possible of the role imbalanced brain chemistry may be playing in the person's life.

Here is what Beth's checklist revealed:

Brain Subsystem (some of this will be a review)	Score	Interpretation
Temporal Lobes The temporal lobes, or the "sides" of the brain, help a person control moods, as well as interpret tone of voice and facial expressions. They also play a role in short- and long-term memory, anxiety, and depression.	6	A score of 6 indicates that the temporal lobes may be playing a role in Beth's problems. Any score greater than five indicates abnormal activity in the temporal lobes, which leads to struggles with mood swings and volatility.

Basal Ganglia The basal ganglia act like anxiety thermostats. Healthy basal ganglia help people feel physically relaxed, positive, and able to deal with conflict.	14	When a person scores 5 or above, a consulting psychiatrist will evaluate for medication. At 14, Beth's entire body is at a "fight or flee" level of threat.
Cingulate The cingulate can be compared to a gear shifter. It helps people move from one emotion or thought to another and enables them to be flexible and cooperative. A healthy cingulate also allows people to see options for their present and future behavior.	7	Because a score of 5 or more indicates cingulate malfunctioning, Beth's score of 7 implies that when she locks on to negative or self-punishing messages, it becomes extraordinarily difficult for her get "unstuck." Beth's overactive cingulate causes her extreme difficulty in calming down enough to take positive steps when she feels like injuring herself.
Deep Limbic System This portion of the brain controls mood, sleep, appetite, and sexual cycles. It also aids in the processing of emotionally charged memories.	9	Beth's limbic score suggests that she is depressed, may be having trouble sleeping or eating, and probably battles feelings of hopelessness and despair.
Prefrontal Cortex Considered the "chief executive" of the brain, the prefrontal cortex controls, among other things, impulse control, attention, concentration, judgment, forethought, planning, and conscience.	15	Any score higher than 9 indicates problems in the executive functioning of the brain. Beth's score of 15 leads me to believe that she functions under unhealthy impulsivity and lack of discernment, and swings from high energy to sluggish spaciness, all of which results from a prefrontal cortex that needs medical attention.

As you can see, Beth's checklist scores indicated that brain chemistry played a significant role in her problems. Sharing the results with Beth, I explained how her brain's overactivity made it difficult to deal with the pain and shame of her many "secrets." Given her results, I encouraged Beth to do a SPECT study.

Beth's SPECT scan looked like this:

Beth's SPECT Scan

Used by permission, courtesy of the Amen Clinic

Here we see what is called decreased perfusion in Beth's prefrontal cortex. Under times of stress, this makes it difficult for Beth to say no to self-injurious impulses. As we've noted, the PFC helps control attention, concentration, judgment, and forethought. Forethought—the ability to think through and see the consequence of an action—is hindered by an underactive PFC. It is difficult for Beth to have forethought under stress.

Beth's concentration SPECT study shows scalloping. This top-down view looks more like the surface of the moon, when it should be nice and smooth.

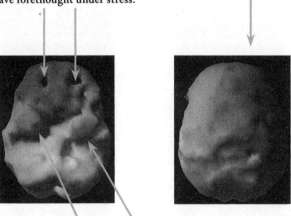

There are changes in both Beth's left and right temporal lobes. This helps explain the problems Beth has with controlling her moods. The temporal lobes play a significant role in relationships. Instability in the temporal lobes can result in people like Beth interpreting words, tone of voice, and facial expressions as being primarily negative or critical.

Beth's SPECT Scan

Used by permission, courtesy of the Amen Clinic

Here we see Beth's right basal ganglia, one of the "anxiety thermo-stats" for her body. Beth's brain is overworking in this area, which has caused significant inflammation. As we can see by looking at the diffuse limbic activity, Beth struggles with mood swings and may battle depression. And by evaluating her cingulate, we see the source of Beth's troubles with obsession and negativity. Sometimes doctors prescribe medications such as Prozac or Effexor to help combat depression and obsessive thoughts. Both drugs are helpful for such symptoms. But these specific medications can also cause the basal ganglia to be even more overstimulated. This often results in increased self-destructiveness. Using a SPECT scan helped Beth's doctors avoid this potentially devastating side effect.

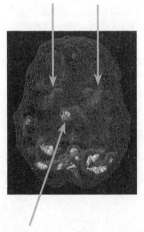 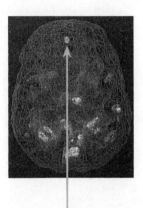

Beth's deep limbic system (DLS) shows diffuse activity, which indicates that her mood, sleep, and sexual cycles will be disturbed. This will also affect her appetite. The deep limbic system is where depression and emotionally charged memories lie, and knowing Beth's history of abuse and her current mood swings, these results help me understand the role DLS chemistry is playing in her life.

Beth's cingulate is significantly inflamed and overactive. Looking at this helps me understand why it is difficult for Beth to "let go" of self-destructive thoughts. With a cingulate as hot as hers, it's no wonder Beth overfocuses on negative, worrisome, and anxiety-producing sensations.

Beth's scan indicated to supervising psychiatrists—and to me—that as well as psychological therapy, she was clearly in need of chemical, nutritional, and supplemental interventions that could help her break her self-injurious patterns.

Beth's biochemical challenges did not remove responsibility for her actions, but it did help her recognize that biological issues contributed significantly to her long-term problem with self-abuse. Knowing that her overactive emotions were not "all in her head," Beth began to release the guilt she had felt for her self-injurious behavior and unstable mental condition.

As she faced her physiological challenges head-on, Beth could better see that attempting to manage the traumatic memories and experiences of her childhood abuse, "cutting out" internal pain, and trying to fill the void inside her with sexual relationships would not work forever.

The trauma Beth experienced as a child most likely created and perpetuated physiological changes in her brain, indicated by the high scores on her Subsystems Checklist and the results of her SPECT scan. Vulnerable chemistry—which we defined earlier as the innate temperament and physical makeup that keeps some people from learning to deal with mental anguish—may have played a role as well, but because of Beth's experience with childhood sexual abuse, it is virtually impossible to discern how large a part (if any) genetic factors played.

By following through with her medical therapy, as well as confronting the spiritual and emotional shame that further destroyed her, Beth started to live without self-injury on a day-to-day basis. I'm happy to report that Beth continues to live in the freedom that attending to her body and soul afforded her.

A RIPPLE EFFECT

Right after my first car accident, I couldn't stop the images, emotions, and sensations I had experienced from flooding into my mind. In the quiet stillness of the night as I lay in my bed, sleep eluded me. I replayed the experience over and over again.

Eventually, the memories faded and my feelings became less intense. Without even noticing, I moved on and put the experience behind me. As it did for me, this natural "replay" mechanism in the human brain usually helps a person process emotionally charged events.

My car accident was a relatively mild form of trauma. But extremely traumatizing experiences—being caught in a natural disaster or life-threatening accident; attacked in war; raped; or physically, verbally, or sexually abused—can rarely be effectively processed in a normal, healthy way.

You may have observed that some victims process tragedy in less time and with seemingly less energy than others who experience the same thing. They appear to work through things, forgive, and move on. Some people, on the other extreme, battle traumatic memories with unrelentingly brutal intensity.

No one's long-term memory is instantaneously formed. Instead, following a given event, information is slowly organized in our brain and then placed into a relatively permanent state through a process called memory consolidation. But during this progression, memories may be modified, especially if the experience included significant emotional stimulation (through fear, anger, a sense of helplessness, and so forth).

Studies performed by neurobiologist Dr. Larry Cahill and his colleagues at facilities like the Center for the Neurobiology of Learning and Memory (at the University of California–Irvine) strongly suggest that the amygdala, our brain's "alarm system," takes physical information and stores the combination of fearful and sensory experiences in a special kind of memory, where data is shaped and layered based on emotionally charged sensations. Dr. Cahill claims the amygdala actually "modulates—or *amplifies*—memory storage . . . when an experience is emotionally arousing."[9]

In addition, the hippocampus, another area of the brain that normally helps integrate information into short- and long-term memory, sometimes malfunctions while attempting to make sense of trauma-imprinted memories and the overwhelming physiological stress those memories retrigger.

Dr. Bessel van der Kolk's research indicates that in people trying to process traumatic memories, the hippocampus is actually significantly smaller than in "normal" subjects. He theorizes that the hippocampus may shrink due to the consistent release of cortisol by the body's stress-response system. At increased levels, cortisol can be toxic to the brain.

An overactive amygdala and underfunctioning hippocampus prevent traumatic events from being processed analytically or dispassionately. Instead of seeing an ordeal as a painful event in their past, some victims of abuse or survivors of war and catastrophe reexperience the horror as a persistent, ongoing, and *present* threat.

Vivid sensations associated with the trauma—smells, sounds, waves of intense fear—wash over these people repeatedly, causing their entire stress-response system (from the brain through the entire body) to become stuck in a state of constant high alert.

Dr. Amen often sees this pattern in self-injurers. And Marilee Strong describes it brilliantly: "Lit up like a pinball machine, all their internal bells and whistles blaring, [traumatized self-harmers] cannot articulate how they feel because they cannot decipher the messages that their nervous system is sending them. Eventually, just having a feeling, any feeling, can seem enormously threatening."[10]

Some attempt to compensate for this continuously heightened state of anxiety by turning off their emotional spigots. They use mood-altering substances (such as alcohol, drugs, or food) or mood-altering behaviors (such as promiscuous sex, binging, purging, starvation, cutting, or burning) to numb their minds and bodies.

SO WHAT CAN WE DO?

I know this feels like an overwhelming amount of information and an impossibly complex number (or combination) of possibilities, but there are some practical things you can do to help self-injurers you care about address the biochemical factors that afflict them.

Though we will discuss many of the following in forthcoming chapters, I would like to introduce several of the ways you can coach self-harmers to combat physiological difficulties that spark and perpetuate self-inflicted violence.

Work with knowledgeable physicians.

Whether self-wounders see a medical doctor, psychiatrist, neurobiologist, or any combination of these three, you can help them make sure that the doctors they work with know about self-injury, including the brain functioning and chemical imbalance that may lead to and propagate it. Encourage them that though finding the right physicians may be a lengthy process, working with doctors who can treat self-harm effectively often makes a *significant* difference in recovery.

Investigate all the options.

There's much more available than just office visits, fill-in-the-blank evaluations, and even CAT scans. When I suffered from a second severe postpartum depression, Dr. Henslin introduced me to the Amen Clinic and the idea of SPECT scanning. The psychiatrists at Dr. Amen's clinic who read my scan recommended medication and nutritional therapy specifically for the overfunctioning and underfunctioning areas of my brain. Rather than prescribing psychotropic drugs in a trial-and-error fashion (which, sadly, is still the modus operandi these days), they recommended meds appropriate for my needs. They also informed me of cognitive recovery options (for example, "talk" therapy, biofeedback, and EMDR, a treatment method involving eye movement). Other brain imaging practices and therapy may be available in your area. I recognize that for some people, whether because of cost, health insurance, or where they live, options like SPECT imaging are not available. Please allow me to reemphasize that no one method of diagnosis or treatment is *absolutely* necessary. Recovery is possible within the means the self-injurer you care about has. It is possible to believe this statement because people of every economic station and living condition have battled and overcome self-harm. We simply want to present as many of the potential methods of treatment as we can in as clear and comprehensive a manner as possible.

Use medication when necessary.

Medication alone does not "cure" problems that result from both psychiatric and behavioral factors (like self-harm). But it may prove a tremendously effective adjunct to medical attention and therapy. For some patients with serotonin deficiencies, SSRI (Selective Serotonin Reuptake Inhibitor) drugs like Prozac and Paxil have significantly decreased self-injurious impulses. Opiate blockers like Naltrexone have helped many self-wounders in the recovery process. And during studies using antiseizure medicines like Tegretol and Lamictal—which stabilize mood through calming the cingulate, temporal lobes, and basal ganglia—no serious acts of self-injury occurred. Some "anxiolytics prevent the escalation of panic and generalized anxiety, which decreases the need for dissociation and self-injury."[11] In these ways, psychotropic drugs can provide a kind of "pharmacological safety net" that allows people to process past memories and current experiences without becoming overwhelmed. You can help self-harmers see that there is no shame in addressing the body's physical needs. All of us would encourage loved ones to take medicine that would help control their diabetes or high blood pressure. Having vulnerable mental chemistry is no different from having any other physiological condition. Tragically, the stigma (often faith-based) attached to mental disease prevents many people from seeking the treatment that would help them overcome destructive impulses and biochemical states that perpetuate self-injurious behavior. Anyone who comes alongside a self-harmer should work to prevent this form of shame from stalling his or her recovery.

Include nutritional therapy.

Most of us recognize that when we eat well, we feel better. Self-injurers are no different. A diet high in protein (including soy products and fish), whole grains, and vegetables gives the nervous system the nutritional support necessary to combat self-wounding impulses. Certain foods actually stimulate the production of serotonin or dopamine. A trained nutritionist, medical doctor, or psychiatrist can help a self-harmer develop an appropriate dietary plan.

Make vitamins and supplements a part of recovery.
Taking brain-boosting vitamins and supplements (especially omega-3 fatty acids and Vitamin E) may help a self-injurer's mind and body be better prepared to deal with urges to self-harm. Sometimes vitamins and supplements can actually decrease these cravings.

Acknowledge that thoughts and beliefs can significantly influence physical health.
The things people dwell on throughout the day encourage or discourage not only their mental well-being but their physical health as well. Bitter, anxious, or angry people tend to suffer from physical problems such as increased heart rate and blood pressure, stomach problems, headaches, and so forth. Recurrent negative thinking or obsessive perfectionism can also instigate and then perpetuate these problems, as well as clinical depression. We can help self-injurers process the thoughts that shape every aspect of them—body, mind, and spirit.

HARDWIRED DOES NOT MEAN DESTINED
People often fear that suffering from innate chemical imbalance (being hardwired with the propensity toward mental disorder) sentences them to permanent psychological problems.

But this is far from true. The same genetically inherited traits can take different forms in different people, depending on circumstances, upbringing, and an individual's commitment to care for the mind, body, and soul.

A self-injurer may never "recover" from vulnerable chemistry, but he or she can recover from the symptomatic behaviors that result from physical makeup. Recognizing your body's needs, meeting them whenever possible, and teaching people in your life to do the same goes a long way in promoting both physical well-being and mental health.

5 HOW WILL YOU KNOW?
Understanding the Messages Self-Injurers Send

A DAD SPEAKS OUT

My son Ryan deliberately and repetitively burns himself.

And you know, even though our family has been battling this for a few months, it's still hard for me to acknowledge, let alone understand why, he does this.

When Ryan turned sixteen, my wife and I noticed some distressing changes in his attitude and appearance. Ryan was what you might call a late bloomer, so we kind of assumed that his "I only want to wear black" and "Just see if you matter to me" posture was a teenage phase, part of your typical adolescent boundary testing.

Our home had always been a pretty happy one. I mean, we're not perfect, but we love one another. Janet and I are proud of our kids. We talk about them all the time and only stopped showing people their pictures when they demanded we do so.

Until Ryan entered high school, we spent time together as a family every week. I taught my boys to surf and play field hockey. Janet handled the homework bit (I never did get geometry), and the boys excelled in school, even with sports and other activities. We went to the movies and ate way too much popcorn and far too many Skittles and then laughed at how ridiculous most Hollywood plots turned out to be.

Things got harder when Ryan's older brother Jason went into eleventh grade. The stresses of SATs and a more demanding academic schedule, as well as new social dynamics (when did prom become such a big deal?) definitely stole from our family time. We went out less, brought out the sticks and goals to practice less. Looking back, I realize we started talking less.

Ryan dropped out of field hockey in the middle of his season. I was disappointed and he knew it. But he didn't seem to care that much. His moods could swing from low to high to lowest within an hour. About the same time, new friends started coming around, friends that I tried to like, despite their different hair and dress. They were actually pretty polite, and it had always been harder for Ryan to make friends, so I let things slide here and there.

Maybe I should have tried harder to stay close to Ryan during those couple of months. I don't know. Even if it made his self-injury my fault, I think I would rather have a reason that explained why he would sear himself with cigarette lighters. It just seems too crazy.

We found out Ryan was burning himself on a Saturday morning. I remember it so clearly. I can still taste my anger and shock and *fear*.

Ryan had to attend Saturday school that day because he'd been caught with a cigarette lighter at school. We talked to him about smoking, but he persisted with the lie that he was just holding on to the lighter for a friend.

The morning of his detention, Ryan sat down at the breakfast table and reached for the cereal box. As he stretched toward Captain Crunch, the long sleeve of his shirt inched up to above his elbow. I noticed two circular burns on Ryan's upper forearm, burns that couldn't have happened by accident.

Without even thinking, I grabbed his wrist and said, "Ryan, what happened?" He ripped his arm out of my hand and said, "It's nothing, Dad. I burned myself on the stove yesterday."

"You don't get round burns from a stove, Ryan." I could feel my temperature rising and my concern mounting. For some reason the words "Let me see your other arm" fell out of my mouth.

"No!" he practically screamed.

"Ryan!" I barked through clenched teeth. Thank God, I stopped, took a deep breath, and said as calmly as I could, "Son, please show me your arm."

In a motion that could have been either resignation or defiance, he pushed the sleeve of his shirt up. Six burns, each the same size, each with concentric, diminutive circles, lined his arm from elbow to wrist.

It took everything inside me not to yell. Instead, I croaked in a broken voice, "Ryan, what in the world is going on? Did you do this to yourself?"

A horn honked. Ryan's ride was here. He grabbed his backpack and slammed the door. I stared at the space his burned arm had just occupied. I ached. I raged. I had no idea what to do. In a haze of conflicting emotions, I picked up the phone and dialed my wife's cell number. Janet answered cheerfully, "Hey, sweetie. What's up?"

"You need to come home. Ryan's . . ." My voice trailed off. I just couldn't bring myself to say it.

"Randy? Randy, what's wrong? What's going on?"

"Just come home, honey."

MY DAUGHTER'S WEBRINGS

Like Ryan's father did, a hardworking and devoted single mom also discovered that her child regularly self-harms. This mother shared her confusing and painful experience online:

I just found out this week that my 14-year-old daughter is a "cutter." She has a 4.0 average, . . . goes to a good school, and is well-liked by all who know her. She is popular, has two homes (mine and her dad's) with supportive, loving families in each. . . .

[Still,] my daughter cuts herself with a safety pin. I found this out on her own personal website, which I discovered she had been hiding on a hidden account she used at another relative's home. She had links to webrings about cutting, suicide and broken hearts as well as images and poetry. Her friends all feature cutting-suicide links, icons and song lyrics as well.

The counselor at her school told me this: At her middle school, "70 percent of the kids here cut or know someone who does. It's cool, a trend, and acceptable. Boys do it as well, but are more public about it . . . you're not even the first parent this week: you're the third, and just today a girl received stitches in the hospital for cutting herself so bad."[1]

WATCHING, WEIGHING, AND WISDOM

Fortunately for those of us who desire to help, self-injurers often give us clues to their behavior. Like Ryan's dad and the mom who shared her story online, family members and loved ones like you can help uncover secretive self-wounding by identifying common warning signs. These signals range from what some might see as obvious to complex and difficult-to-discern behaviors that can simultaneously indicate a number of emotional distresses.

Whether you suspect someone you know is caught in a self-injurious cycle or you discovered long ago that a loved one does hurt himself or herself, knowing how to recognize these red flags is invaluable.

Obviously, learning to read signals will be crucial in initially identifying self-wounding behaviors. But because periods of increased pressure or emotional strain can precipitate bouts of self-inflicted vio-lence—even for people committed to recovery—lovingly watching for signs that indicate a resurgence of injurious activities will also prove incredibly important.

One caution before you read on: Though it makes matters more complicated, we show the most love and concern for others when we refrain from assuming that any of the following signs can indisputably prove that a person is hurting himself or herself. Instead of presuming and reacting, we can observe carefully, weigh all the information, and proceed with any action respectfully and mercifully.

In an ideal world, we would neither jump to conclusions nor ignore warning signs. But we do not live in a perfect world; we have not been equipped with flawless discernment. We can, however, seek balance between trust and concern. Of course, this will be challenging, but I truly believe that with patience, clear vision, and commitment to serve the person you are concerned about, you *will* be able to evaluate the following clues and offer help that meets your loved one where he or she is.

With this in mind, here are some signs that may indicate someone you love self-injures or is contemplating self-injury.

Frequent cuts, burns, or bruises are "explained away."

People who self-harm often stockpile excuses for the wounds they cannot hide or choose not to cover or for those that are exposed unexpectedly. Excuses may include, "I cut myself shaving," "I burned myself cook-ing last night," "I got a bite and it just itched so bad I rubbed myself raw," "An animal bit [or scratched] me," and "I ran into something in the dark last night." Some explanations seem absolutely plausible, and self-wounders intent on keeping their habits secret often become ter-rific liars. Still, repeated excuses and recurrent wounds usually point to something more than what they've willingly disclosed. They may be hiding the abuse another inflicts upon them, or they may be disguising self-inflicted injuries.

Clothing seems ill-fitting or ill-suited for the climate or season.

A person who wears long sleeves or pants all summer or someone who refuses to don a bathing suit or a pair of shorts may be hiding scars, cuts, or burns. Those who wear excessively loose or baggy clothing may do so to prevent fabric from touching fresh wounds. While we cannot assume that every fashion choice indicates a self-harming behavior (we all know that baggy and loose clothes are sometimes considered stylish), we can evaluate patterns and watch for a combination of this and other warning signs.

The person demonstrates a reluctance to change or try on clothes in front of someone else.

With careful attention, you can often tell the difference between a modest person who simply wants privacy, someone who feels uncomfortable with his or her body (see next point), and someone who is hiding his or her body for other reasons. Without pressing too hard, yet simultaneously noting any other warning signs, you may be able to uncover why someone does not want others to see his or her bare skin.

The person appears to have strong body dissatisfaction.

Many people, especially women, dislike (even feel disgusted by) their bodies. But people who self-injure will usually take this to an extreme. They often express malevolence toward their physique, feeling their bodies have betrayed or disappointed them. And since self-inflicted violence and eating disorders are often concurrently present, warning signs of anorexia, bulimia, or binge eating disorder—including but not limited to marked weight loss or gain, evidences of binging and purging through the use of diuretics and laxatives, and strange eating habits or rituals—may simultaneously signal a person's use of self-harm to cope with intense body dissatisfaction.

There is intense resistance to routine doctor visits or to seeking medical attention for wounds that clearly need treatment.

Few children like to visit the doctor. But by adolescence, most young people have outgrown the toddler's "throw a fit because I have to get a checkup" stage. Even those who fear hospitals and doctors' offices can usually be cajoled (or forced) into keeping necessary appointments. If someone obstinately and inexplicably refuses to see a physician, whether for a preventive appointment or during an illness, a deeper problem may exist. In addition, self-injurers who inadvertently cut or burn themselves too deeply may excuse their injury, say they'll be okay without stitches or medical attention, and think this sufficient to "throw you off the trail." If you push for a trip to the doctor or emergency room, the self-harmer may refuse—vehemently. The teenager or young adult, even the adult spouse or family friend who intentionally wounds himself or herself may fear discovery so much that he or she would rather suffer the consequences of untreated injuries than be found out. Keep this in mind if someone stubbornly refuses to see a physician.

The person wears accessories to cover the skin.

Some people will use watches, wristbands, or bracelets to cover their scars or recent cuts/burns. If you are concerned about someone, demanding that he or she remove accessories probably won't help. Instead, watch for times when the skin is exposed and ask nonthreatening questions that open the door for your friend/child/student to talk (for example, "It looks like you hurt yourself; what happened?," "You have a cut on your wrist. Would you like me to bandage that for you?," or "That looks painful. Did that happen recently?"). Some self-wounders actually want people to notice and give them the freedom or a reason to communicate.

There are clusters of similar markings on the body.

Since other self-injurers will do virtually anything to keep their behavior secret, carefully created cuts/scratches/burns may not initially look like intentional, repetitive wounds. But if you notice that red, irritated, or otherwise irregular marks on the skin continue to appear, a person may be experimenting with self-inflicted violence.

The person's friends self-injure.

While most people do not start self-injuring simply because others they know do (remember, a person who decides to copy such an extreme coping mechanism is usually suffering from his or her own unaddressed emotional pain), there is an observable contagion factor in certain circles. If a young man or woman's peer group—whether at church, school, or on the Internet—defines itself through self-destructive behaviors, or if a person witnesses cutting/burning as accomplishing a desired result, he or she may be at a higher risk for self-harm.

A normally outgoing person withdraws from family and friends.

A shift in personality like this almost always indicates a problem, whether it be something as normal as disappointment in relationships or part of a more serious issue such as self-injury, depression, or suicidal ideation.

Dramatic mood swings occur in a short time frame.

If you continually observe someone you love swinging from high tension to a more relaxed state in a very short period of time, you may want to find out what happened to cause the change. Self-wounders can be noticeably anxious or distraught at 5:00 p.m. and emerge from the bathroom or their room at 5:30, apparently feeling much better. What happened in that half hour? A healthy person may have had a nice hot shower or a phone call from a friend. A person who exhibits any of the other warning signs listed in this chapter, however, may be using self-inflicted violence to release pent-up frustration or sadness.

The person continually uses language that expresses low self-worth or the need to be punished.

Most people who injure themselves struggle with forming an accurate and gracious view of themselves. They may talk about being bad or needing to make up for their mistakes. Try to listen carefully to people's descriptions of self and their place in the world. Additionally, as noted earlier, many self-harmers also battle eating disorders. Excessive conversation about weight, exercise, or food may signal not only a disturbance in dietary health but also a body dislike that could lead to cutting or burning.

The person displays continuous outbursts of anger, tears, or extreme emotion.
Most people who self-injure are trying to figure out how to deal with their emotions. They may not be skilled in verbal expression, and instead of discussing an issue with perspective and calm, self-wounders can blow up at little things, dissolve into tears over a relatively insignificant matter, or display other dramatic emotions ill-suited to the issue at hand.

The family has a history of mental-health issues.
Thankfully, people whose family members battle mental-health problems are not destined to fight the same conditions. It is important, however, to be aware of risk factors. If a close family member struggles with depression, anxiety, or another chemical imbalance, a person may be more likely to try—and eventually depend on—unhealthy coping mechanisms like self-harm.

You find hidden stashes of gauze, bandages, sharp instruments, or other implements that could be used to self-injure or soothe a self-injurious wound.
Most people don't hoard or hide Band-Aids or razors. If you come across a secret supply of items that could be used to inflict harm on oneself or ease the pain of a self-inflicted wound, this is a very good indication that someone you love struggles with self-injury.

Someone else tells you that your friend/spouse/student/child self-injures.
If someone informs you that a loved one self-harms, please do not ignore the warning. *Ever.* Even in the rarest cases when a third party maliciously invents such a story, a relational and communication problem

clearly needs to be addressed. Most of the time, however, when people tell you that someone you love injures himself or herself, they do so because it is (or at least has been) true. Self-injury is *not* something that simply goes away with time. Take seriously any information about self-inflicted violence that someone brings to your attention.

Again, allow me to remind you that none of these signals irrefutably "proves" that someone self-harms. Warning signs such as excessively negative self-perception, body dissatisfaction, dramatic mood swings, and emotional outbursts may crop up in the way a young adult (or a premenstrual woman, an unemployed man, and so on) processes the changes in his or her body, mind, and world.

A person you love may also be depressed or anxious but not self-injurious. A person you care for may hate his or her body but not cross the line to cutting or burning. Wisdom resists overinterpretation. You can best honor those you love by observing the signs, praying diligently, opening the door for others to share their struggles, and confronting behaviors when needed.

If it ultimately comes to light that someone you love does self-injure or has returned to self-inflicted violence, it would be best to proceed with neutral, nonthreatening discussions. I know this is difficult, especially if you are emotionally invested in this person. But demands and angry responses will not ingratiate a wounded self-harmer to you. These conversations require gentleness and patience.

Evasive responses ("Oh, it's nothing" and "I've only done it once") will be common. Still, you can lovingly probe, letting a person know that you won't take his or her behavior, even "infrequent" cuts or "minor" burns, lightly.

The more effectively and consistently you evaluate warning signs and eventually confront self-injury, the better the chance that you can be part of a healthy and lasting recovery. And if you can catch a problem or a resurgence early on through keen observation and a desire to find out what is really going on (without excessive intrusiveness), all the better.

GENERAL "CATEGORIES" OF SELF-INJURERS' MOTIVATIONS

If, or when, you discover that someone you know self-harms, it may be helpful to look at the following "categories" (and I use that term very loosely because people—self-harmers included—never fit perfectly into any grouping) of individuals who tend to inflict violence on themselves in order to communicate, calm inner pain, and so forth. The following phrases express some of the emotions that motivate self-wounders.

"Notice me."

The only attention Amber got at home ranged from negative to abusive. Her mom constantly picked on her about her weight, the cleanliness of her room, and her "bad attitude." Amber's dad went beyond verbal berating. When something didn't meet his standards, when Amber "forgot her place," he would hit her, but never severely enough to leave marks others could identify. Still, Amber's dad struck hard enough to hurt, inside and out.

Amber started a pattern of self-injury by binging and purging on "forbidden" foods (cookies, candy, chips, and so on). From her experimentation with bulimia, it seemed a short stretch for Amber to harm herself in other ways. So she began cutting her skin.

I found out about Amber's behavior in a letter she wrote and gave to me in strict confidence. But because I felt legally and personally obligated to inform someone about her self-injurious behaviors, I spoke with my husband, who is a pastor, and his women's ministry assistant. That was when I discovered I was not the only person Amber had shared her "deepest, darkest secret" with.

Amber had already confided her self-harming patterns to both of the people I shared them with, as well as to a couple of other leaders in the youth ministry and a professional therapist she had seen for a short time. Each time she confessed to an adult mentor, Amber received an outpouring of love and support. But once her counselor and the youth group volunteers and staff asked her to take steps toward healing, Amber balked and then moved on to someone else.

Amber wanted people to know. But because she talked about rather than hid her self-injury, would I call her a phony? *No way.* Amber simply believed that some loving attention is better than none. She used the "secret" of her very real self-harm to draw others in.

At the same time, Amber didn't want to be challenged. She found pursuing healing more difficult than simply sharing her secret. And commanding the attention of others, even manipulating their emotions, stood in sharp contrast to the helplessness and inattention she experienced at home.

Like Amber, some self-injurers long to be noticed. And as we identified previously, they are attention-*needing* (as opposed to merely attention-seeking). Amber's emotional tank had been running on empty for years. She craved the consideration and love of others. And she used self-injury to both quiet the pain of her abusive home and get others to notice her.

Some "notice me" self-harmers may be more dramatic than Amber, even to the point of being exhibitionists. They damage themselves in full view of the world. And the intensely focused fear, worry, and anger that others express often reinforce their self-inflicted violence, simply because the attention they receive while self-injuring is preferable to the love deficit they usually live with.

Other self-wounders who want or need attention injure themselves for peer recognition. Some, especially those involved in Goth[2] or Emo[3] circles, almost brag about their cutting or burning. This false bravado should not be treated as another form of "teenage melodrama." One San Diego therapist recommends that parents take "notice me" self-injurers like this to the emergency room, where self-inflicted violence is *not* a cool or fashionable thing but rather a sign of mental-emotional disturbance.

Again, "notice me" cutters aren't fakers. Even if it looks as if a teenager self-injures primarily because his or her peer group does, self-inflicted violence of any kind reveals maladaptive social and emotional coping mechanisms and, moreover, a person who needs help.

Consider the experience of Katie, the heroine of Steven Levenkron's book *The Luckiest Girl in the World*. When someone saw her scars and didn't comment, "Katie couldn't believe it. Nothing was going to happen. For some reason, that made her want to cry."[4]

"Notice me" self-injurers need attention and loving care, even if they don't initially or outwardly show it. And once you've identified "notice me" behaviors in self-harmers, you can begin to help them see their value and uniqueness apart from self-injury. You can help them see that they are special, not because they self-harm but because God created them to be so.

"I can't feel anything" or "I feel too much."

People who self-injure often use self-inflicted violence to "ground" themselves. Grounding is a term that describes a complex and sometimes subconscious psychological motivation for self-injury. By cutting, burning, breaking, or bruising the body, self-harmers "ground" or reestablish themselves in reality.

Remember, for those who have buried their internal pain so long they can feel few, if any, emotions at all, self-injurious behaviors allow them to feel physically what they cannot sense or explain emotionally.

Patricia McCormick's novel *Cut* chronicles the experience of Callie, an "I can't feel anything" self-injurer who says, "An ache fills my chest. I want something, but I can't put a name to it."[5] A gnawing despair, a continual but unidentified unease, plagues Callie. She feels miserable but can't identify what she longs for or why. When she cuts, she can finally point to some "thing" that causes and makes visible her pain.

On the flip side, those who feel too much—those who revisit the agony of abuse, the toxicity of rage, the bitterness of unforgiveness, the anguish of anxiety, and/or the despair of depression over and over again—use self-injury to quiet the overwhelming and uncontrollable torrent inside. Grounding enables some self-harmers to escape from, if only momentarily, the tidal wave of pain that threatens to swallow them.

Ruth, Melody Carlson's verbally abused "I feel too much" heroine, starts *Blade Silver* with these tragic words: "Sometimes I feel like I'm about to explode. Or maybe I will implode. I'm not really sure, but I think it's going to get messy. And I think someone's going to get hurt. Probably me."[6]

Instead of exploding or imploding around or at others, Ruth retreats to her bathroom, where she grounds herself with a razor, gauze, and bandages. When she emerges from what she sees as the "safe place" of self-injury, Ruth feels better able (though only temporarily) to face the pain of her everyday life. She expresses, "It's like it's my only source of control. And then there's the pain. The never-ending pain that seems only to be diminished by pain. Pain erasing pain. And yet it never really goes away. Sometimes the only answer seems to be to cut deeper."[7]

After identifying those who use self-injury to ground themselves, you can help them find alternative methods of feeling or facing their internal pain. We will discuss this at length in chapters 7 and 8.

"Show no weakness."

Perfectionism places *extreme* pressure on the mind, body, and spirit of an individual. Some high achievers and people pleasers attempt to diffuse the constant tension of human imperfection with self-inflicted violence. This group of self-harmers fears being "discovered" or "exposed" as weak or lacking. Some loathe failure so much that they would rather die than taste the disappointment of underachievement or broken relationships.

I have struggled with perfectionism a great deal of my life. And while I did not cut or burn myself, I used another form of self-injury (disordered eating and exercise) to keep my fear of failure and exposure at bay.

For years, I worried more than anything that if people found out what I was "really" like, they would despise me as much as I hated myself at the time. I obeyed the mantra of one sports drink slogan, which claimed, "Better to wound your body than your pride."

But living by this and other self-destructive perfectionistic rules sapped joy from my life. I found it difficult, if not impossible, to accept love and care from others. Because I felt so unworthy of their concern, any approval or praise they communicated never sank in. I discounted the positive expressions of others by keeping my "real, flawed" self under close scrutiny.

So caught up in proving my worth, I found no lasting joy in accomplishments or the compliments that accompanied achievement. I simply plunged myself into the next project, fearing that if I let anything drop, I'd be exposed for the failure I felt I was.

Another self-proclaimed perfectionist, Caroline Kettlewell, writes,

> I [lived] for my GPA because it was something you could count on [but] I got a D once on a short paper . . . and I spent the rest of the day seriously considering killing myself over it. Suicide! Over some crappy one-pager for a course I can't even call to mind anymore. Well, imagine having to live with that Caroline day in and day out. You might be inclined to go for the razor, too, just to shut her up.[8]

Beneath the carefully constructed facade of achievement, most perfectionists feel anything but special. On the contrary, worthlessness and fear often control them. They live rigid, black-and-white, good-or-bad lives that leave them acutely sensitive to criticism or perceived failure. Being adequate is an insult to the "show no weakness" self-injurer.

Other self-wounders use self-inflicted violence to process the unrealistic, pressurized expectations of others. Ashley, a repetitive self-injurer being treated at the S.A.F.E. Alternatives clinic in Illinois, shared these thoughts from her journal: "At home and at school, others think I can do everything, and I think they forget that I need care and love just as much as others who aren't so independent. I get angry when I think no one cares for me and start feeling like they view me more as an adult than as the needy child I feel like inside."[9]

Parents often hold on to idealistic, sometimes impossible expectations for their children. Precocious children, children of perfectionists, and children who become perfectionists themselves often struggle under the weight of other people's hopes and dreams for them.

In *Ophelia Speaks: Adolescent Girls Write About Their Search for Self,* Liz Fullerton-Dummit reflects on a particularly strained time in her life, a time when she felt the crushing weight of her mother's ideas of who she should be. She observes, "The concern in [my mom's] eyes was genuine, but painful. The concern wasn't for me. It was for the facade she had created in her mind, the kid she yearned for me to be."[10]

Children who exhibit a high degree of talent or emotional maturity often find that authority figures expect them to grow up too fast, to accomplish too much. When they fail or when they suffer, they may feel utterly alone, unable to ask if it's okay to miss the mark.

Healing from self-inflicted violence that stems from perfectionism—whether self-imposed, resulting from the unrealistic expectations of others, or a combination of both—requires the reordering of a person's inner and outer worlds. Thought patterns need transforming, habits need breaking, and toxic spiritual misunderstandings need conforming to Truth. In our discussion of treatment options and spiritual healing, we will highlight ways to come alongside perfectionists who cut, burn, bruise, or break instead of embracing their humanity, which includes strengths and weaknesses.

"I'm bad" or "I deserve this."

The following story of a young father and tortured self-wounder, Austin, exemplifies the experience of many people who believe they're just giving themselves what they deserve—pain and punishment.

When Austin's parents divorced, he feared that he was to blame. Hadn't his mom always told him that constantly "taunting" his sister Jennifer was "driving her crazy"? Hadn't his dad said they'd all be much happier if Austin and Jennifer were "better behaved"?

Austin's mom and dad took the strain of their relationship out on their kids. They often punished Austin and Jennifer for no clear reason. A sensitive young man, Austin internalized every discipline, experiencing each as a personal condemnation. When his mother left, abandoning her children, Austin believed he had driven her from their home. His father was distant and cold. Austin concluded that he was alone and uncared for and would be forever.

When Austin met Abbey during his freshman year of college, he thought everything would change. Abbey loved him (though he couldn't understand why) and wanted to be with him. But when Abbey missed her period and discovered that she was carrying Austin's baby, the fears of his adolescence came back with greater force than ever.

Austin and Abbey kept their child and got married. And Austin loved his little girl. But he also felt overwhelmed by the new responsibilities of fatherhood and marriage. Quitting college and taking a full-time job to pay for diapers and smashed peas was not quite what he had imagined he'd be doing at age twenty.

Every time he felt the sting of disappointment, fear, or anger, Austin buried it deep inside. He firmly believed that "bad" feelings and behaviors had pushed his mom from their home and that they might cost him Abbey and their baby too. He tried to reason his emotions away: *I love them. I shouldn't feel like this.*

Still, the thoughts assaulted Austin. So after every onslaught, he punished himself by mercilessly burning his skin on the stove at work. He found that the intense physical pain drove away his shame and fear.

After some time, Abbey confronted Austin about his burns. She cried with him and made an appointment for the two of them to see a counselor. In the first session, Austin expressed that "knowing Abbey loves me and not feeling worthy of it is really hard. It's overwhelming to sense her love, because I just don't deserve it."

Tragically, like Austin, victims of childhood trauma (such as divorce and abuse) often falsely believe themselves responsible for the suffering they experienced. Abusers sometimes tell their victims that they deserve maltreatment because of their "bad [or evil or wrong]" behaviors, feelings, or thoughts.

And in a strange way, blaming themselves for abuse or trauma allows victims to feel a measure of control, as well as identify a concrete reason for the pain in their life. As destructive as this manner of thinking may be, many find it preferable to the terror of believing they are at the mercy of unmanageable, even wicked, forces.

Self-punishers often frame their life around "If only I had . . .," "I should have . . .," or "If only I hadn't . . ." statements. "I deserve this" self-injurers also use self-deprecating words to beat themselves up. Phrases like "I'm lazy," "I'm stupid," "I'm bad," or "I'm crazy" plague the minds of these self-harmers. Yet these same people are usually at a loss for an explicit example that could confirm how wretched they believe they "really are."

Some self-wounders punish themselves for being "different" from, devalued by, or "less than" others. This idea may have been communicated by people around them, or it may stem primarily from unloving self-perception. Often this faulty conclusion is drawn from a combination of both factors.

Grant never felt like part of his family. His older brothers were athletic and outgoing, just like his parents. Grant liked to read and preferred to be with one or two people rather than at the center of a large group.

His mom and dad felt devastated after discovering that Grant burned himself with a cigarette lighter whenever he felt "different" or, as he put it, "rejected." Grant believed that only success and achievement made someone worthwhile in his family. "They don't know what to value in me," Grant concluded.

But his mom and dad expressed the opposite during counseling. They said, "Grant thinks we love him less than his brothers, but it's not true. It's just harder for us to understand him. We don't know what to do."

Grant, radically different from the rest of his family, needed to feel included, valued, loved. His parents literally had to learn how to show their youngest son his worth. Through the process, they also helped the whole family to differentiate between the celebration of success and the cherishing of individual family members simply for being who they are.

If a child senses that he or she is an "outsider" in his or her family, self-inflicted violence may act as a punishment ("I'm not who I should be") or a release ("I can ignore the pain of rejection—perceived or real—if I injure myself"). For "I deserve this" self-harmers, recovery will include extensive internal reprogramming. Self-punishers can start by asking how they came to believe that they were worthy not of love, but only of pain. They can investigate who and what played a role in developing the thoughts and feelings that led and continue to lead to self-injury. And they can explore what makes them valuable and worthy of nurturance rather than negligence, grace rather than grief. You can help them do this by refocusing their conversation, vocabulary, and self-perception on the truths of who they were created to be. You can also pray with wisdom, knowing that self-recrimination forms a huge barrier to love and peace in their lives.

"Better me than someone else."

In *Cut*, Callie, the "good girl" in her family, informs her therapist that she could never tell anyone what she really thinks or feels. The counselor asks, "What's wrong with letting people know what you're doing, or how you're feeling?"

"It's not fair," Callie say[s].

"Not fair?"

"It might upset them."[11]

In Callie's mind, her chronically sick brother is the only one who really needs and deserves attention. She thinks it would be unjust to burden her parents with another problem. Self-injury seems the only way to let her gnawing despair out without infringing on anyone else. She doesn't want to, and resolves she won't, hurt anyone—except herself.

Gary, an incredibly intelligent college student (a physics major, no

INSIDE A CUTTER'S MIND

less), found that deliberately hurting himself temporarily eased the strain his older brother's death placed on his small family. After his brother's tragic car accident, Gary and his parents made a silent but unbreakable agreement never to bring it up. Feeling that his parents would fall apart if he talked about his brother's death, Gary turned to self-injury as a means of coping with unaddressed grief and anger.

Gary absorbed his parents' anguish and combined that weight with the heavy load of personal sorrow he already carried. In an effort to distill his parents' present pain and protect them from further agony, Gary repeatedly hit himself, bruising his hands, arms, and legs.

And though the circumstances differed, twelve-year-old Violet's story, which I came across while reading the accounts of hundreds of self-injurers online, in journals, and in books, mirrors Callie's and Gary's. In Violet's home, when someone got mad, other people got hurt. Anger and physical harm blurred into a single, inextricable category in her mind: Rage equaled acting out.

But because Violet felt that it would be better for her to hurt herself than someone else, especially the parents and siblings she loved, she inflicted violence on herself. More effective in diffusing anger and "safer" (in the sense that only she felt pain) than confronting the person or circumstances that provoked her, Violet's self-injury also became an indirect means of retaliation against her rage-driven parents.

"I'll show them," she seemed to say with each cut. "I'll decide when I get hurt and how much." Yet verbally expressing herself or confessing her self-wounding behaviors was impossible for Violet. Convinced that their anger would boil over and that irreparable damage to their family would be done, Violet kept her repetitive self-inflicted violence a well-guarded secret.

In Gary's and Violet's homes, grieving or angry parents left a nurturance and attention void that sparked self-injurious behavior in their children. Because Callie's mom and dad spent more time and energy on her sickly younger brother, Callie felt it would be unfair to tell her already worried parents that she, too, had a problem that needed help.

If friends or family members cannot offer each other strength, nurturing, and help in processing difficult emotions, they cannot enjoy the security to express the natural negative feelings people inevitably will experience toward one another. Believing that articulating "bad" emotions would leave them alone and loveless, self-wounders "protect" others by inflicting pain only on themselves.

"Better me than someone else" self-injurers clearly display the contradictory nature of self-inflicted violence. They try to "guard" and "shelter" people they love, especially those who are already hurting, but they choose to do it by inflicting more damage. They justify their pain by rationalizing, "It's only me I'm hurting."

Similar to "I deserve this" self-punishers, "better me than someone else" self-injurers can heal best as they learn their own spiritual value. They can also benefit greatly from developing communication skills that allow them to express their own woundedness, even if it causes someone they love discomfort. Opening the door for self-harmers like this to explore all of their emotions, including the uncomfortable ones, will be an important first step on the path to recovery.

All the types of self-injurers we've discussed in this section will find relief in addressing the familial, psychological, and physiological issues that contribute to their self-injury. But, as we know, the process of dissecting and overcoming patterns of self-inflicted violence is not easy.

To genuinely help those we love in the difficult work of recovery, we can all benefit greatly from gaining a clearer understanding of emotional and physical methods of treatment. We'll also find that determining when we can help and when we need to entrust the self-harmers we care about to trained professionals can make a big difference in our ability to persevere in the challenging work of helping someone recover. And finally, we can embrace the spiritual healing that cements hope and wholeness in the human heart. These practical and constructive matters will be discussed throughout the remainder of this book.

6 WHAT CAN I DO?

The Crucial Role You Play in a Self-Injurer's Recovery

Natalie, a dear and cherished friend, recently shared this poem with me:

Cutting

A poem

By Natalie Wiest

Cauterize this wound and I'll be human;
Staunch the flow of needing to be hurt.

Press the cool clean blade against my surface.
Knife out my poisoned blood.

But all the scars still show in the morning,
Even where they don't exist . . .

If you met Natalie, I highly doubt you'd suspect that she inflicts violence on herself. Nat expresses herself well; in fact, she's a gifted communicator. Natalie's an artist who paints life with broad strokes and beautiful texture. And Nat has also battled self-harming impulses for thirteen years. I helped her write the following, a short memoir she entitles "Needing to Be Hurt."

Seventh grade pretty much sucked. Being twelve years old was hard enough, but being completely abandoned by my best friend, feeling like I would never measure up to my suddenly popular, always successful older sister, and generally seeing myself as ugly, fat, and worthless certainly didn't help.

After the girl who had called herself my closest friend, the girl who told me things wouldn't change when she moved, the girl I had used all of my Christmas money to visit six states away totally humiliated me in front of her new and "cooler" friends, I came home and fell apart.

I didn't necessarily want to die, but I desperately needed an escape from the rejection that threatened to swallow me. It probably sounds strange to you, but cutting myself seemed like the only solution. So I did. And it scared me half to death. I stopped as soon as the bright red blood began to flow from my forearms. Honestly, I never thought I'd try it again.

Seven years later, after an extended battle with self-starvation and bulimia, as well as a continual struggle for some kind of healthy self-esteem, I started obsessing about cutting myself. Not about slashing my wrists to make a final exit; just about slicing myself for the sake of cutting. These thoughts both terrified and compelled me. Over the next three or four years, I injured myself sporadically, symbolically, and sometimes savagely.

There wasn't a discernable pattern or rhythm to my cutting. It just depended on what happened in a given day, during a certain week, or over the course of a month. Once, I went for a whole year without cutting myself. Then it started all over again.

If I felt I'd made a fool of myself, if I thought I'd hurt someone I cared about and couldn't do something to fix it, if I made a social blunder or performed poorly, the urge to cut increased. Sometimes I gave in; sometimes I resisted.

I tried to cut away the wicked parts of me. I tried to make up for the bad things I did. I bled the fear of rejection and the ache of failure out of my body. I sliced away at my sensuality and the messiness of my longings.

Usually I cut carefully, in places I could easily hide or cover. But sometimes I cut in places that symbolized or reflected the chaos inside my mind and heart. I cut on my breasts while despising my broken sexuality. I sliced my face when, defying my fear of rejection, I wanted my wounds to scream, "I don't care if you see or what you think."

After a particularly bad episode, I was finally convinced I had to tell someone, so I chose to confide in Rachel, an older girl who didn't strike me as the kind of person who would over-react. Rachel gave me a compassionate, firm hug, prayed with me, and encouraged me to see our university's counselor. I said I would.

It took me awhile to follow through with that promise. During my battle with eating issues, I had some *really* bad experiences with counseling. One psychologist told me I wasn't doing therapy "right." Another basically insisted that I stop immediately or he wouldn't help me. Needless to say, seeing a third counselor didn't thrill me.

But I finally made the appointment and kept it. This time, the therapist I saw acted with mercy and haste. She contacted a psychiatrist to have me evaluated. She phoned my parents, and even though that call scared me more than I could explain, I felt relieved that they finally knew.

After being diagnosed with major depression and recognizing that my eating problems wouldn't go away for good unless I dealt with the root issues, I slowly began to confront my fear of failure and rejection, my poor body image, and the disappointed anger I felt with my family.

Well-meaning as they were, my parents wanted me to just

INSIDE A CUTTER'S MIND

"get over" my self-injurious behaviors and depressed condition. Together, we confronted—and continue to confront—the patterns of broken communication and perfectionistic expectation that contributed to my cutting. And when medical professionals recommended it, we also submitted (me to taking and them to agreeing) to antidepressant medication. Recovery wasn't simply a "work on me" project; it was a "we're all in this together" journey.

During the process, some people were amazingly helpful. One of my college roommates, Cori, and I made a pact that I would tell her whenever I cut and show her when I felt able. Sometimes I agonized even with the thought of keeping our agreement, but Cori didn't judge me, get angry, retreat, or act frightened. I remember the hugs that she would give and the prayers she would cover me with. When I felt ready to talk about it, Cori would listen and help me think through what I could do next. If being alone felt too threatening, she would stay with me.

Other people reacted terribly. My sister flipped out and lectured me for two hours, battering me with Bible verses that "proved" God wouldn't want me to do this to myself. She didn't understand why I couldn't just stop, since I knew cutting was wrong.

When I asked one friend, Blair, to hang out with me because I felt tempted to cut, she got scared . . . and angry. After a drawn-out confrontation, she told me she didn't know what else to say and concluded that maybe I should just cut and get it over with. Blair apologized afterward, but getting derision from the very person I'd turned to for help and support hurt so badly.

If there's one thing I could tell people who want to help self-injurers, it's to look again at the people in your life who wound themselves. Try to imagine what it feels like to wonder if you're crazy, if you'll ever be normal, if you'll ever get better. Try to conceive of a heartache so deep, thoughts so overwhelming, that you can't even find the energy to fight, let alone bring them under control. Then ask yourself how you'd want others to treat you. Ask yourself what kind of help you would want . . . and need.

More than likely, you want to *do* something for the self-injurers you know. But chances are you're not a professional or clinician. Maybe you work at a school where cutting has become rampant. Maybe, like me, you work with young people at church. You may be the parent or spouse or lay counselor of someone who self-injures.

This chapter is for you. We're going to look at what those of us who aren't therapists, psychiatrists, or psychologists can do. In this chapter (and the next) we will discuss many paths to and aspects of recovery. Some may be familiar to you; others may initially strike you as strange. Please look at all these methods with an open mind. The very thing you initially recoil from could be the form of treatment that best helps a self-harmer you love.

LEARNING IN ORDER TO LOVE

Before we jump in, think about the last time you flew on an airplane. We all have heard the flight attendant reminding us that "in case of an emergency, you should first secure your own oxygen mask before helping someone else."

In the same manner, before we can effectively and lovingly help others, it's best to first consider the ways we cope with heartache. Though our natural desire may be to rush to the aid of a wounded person, we cannot model healthy living for a self-injurer if we have never learned how to confront pain.

Fortunately there are some practical ways each of us can evaluate and improve our ability to deal with distress. Authentically facing our own brokenness, we can then provide an example of living without self-harm.

In the following sections, we'll look first at what we can learn. Then we'll process what we can model for the self-wounders we care for. Woven throughout, you'll also find a variety of specific ways that you can encourage people on the path to recovery.

Please keep in mind while you read that you do *not* have to be perfect in order to model healthy living for self-harmers. In fact, the self-wounder you love will need to see that it's okay to make mistakes. None of us can do all the things this chapter suggests. All of us will be better at some things than we are at others. Addressing our own complicated issues or coping mechanisms just helps us to relate better, to view the people we desire to help with compassion instead of judgment, and to watch that our own weaknesses don't infringe on the recovery process.

With that said, here are some important things we can start implementing into our lives.

Getting Comfortable with Uncomfortable Emotions

Like self-injurers, many of us dislike feeling intense emotions. But we do not have to view any feeling—including anger, frustration, guilt, grief, and desire—as "forbidden" or "unacceptable." God has given us a range of emotions with which to express beauty and brokenness (if you doubt this, read the book of Psalms for evidence). Strong emotions almost always accompany the discovery that someone you know struggles with self-inflicted violence. Your anger at, fear of or for, and frustration with a self-harmer are not "bad." In fact, by learning to process and appropriately express these emotions, you will serve self-wounders well.

Allowing Others to Experience Uncomfortable Emotions

Self-harmers often report that their feelings are trivialized or discounted. When upset or frightened, people who express their feelings may be ignored, shamed, or even punished for strong feelings.

In her online "Self Injury Fact Sheet," Deb Martinson reports that "most people who self-injure were chronically invalidated in some way as children (many self-injurers report abuse, but *almost all* report chronic invalidation)."[1]

Children whose parents say things like

- "Stop that crying or I'll give you something to cry about."
- "That's not a big deal. Just suck it up."
- "You shouldn't be afraid of [or hurt by or angry about] that."
- "Big boys [or girls] don't cry like that."
- "Normal people don't feel that way."

often grow up believing that their feelings don't matter. They may doubt their own ability to evaluate or handle their emotions.

Please don't assume that if you've used phrases like these you've caused people in your sphere of influence to self-injure. Rarely is a single person "at fault" in circumstances of self-inflicted violence. Even if you've repetitively said such things (perhaps you were told them as a child yourself), redemption is readily available.

Reversing the flow of emotional trivialization starts with recognizing that all emotions can be valid. Of course, every feeling can be expressed healthily or harmfully, and discerning which is which can be difficult. But anger, fear, guilt, and hurt all have appropriate places in the range of human emotions.

Listening to What Uncomfortable Emotions Say

Both you and the self-harmer you know will benefit from learning to explore what your feelings reveal. Every emotion exposes a belief about the self, reality, and God. As we all know, some of our feelings and the thoughts behind them carry significant and anguished baggage. Self-injury is a quick fix in that it immediately gratifies—by temporarily ending—emotional distress. Choosing not to cut, burn, reach for the bag of chips, purge, drown yourself in work, or do something else to "rid yourself" of uncomfortable feelings means that you have to actually persevere when experiencing emotions like loneliness, loss, rage, remorse, and disillusionment. You also have to confront the poisonous lies that drive you to self-protection and self-abuse. At first, Caroline Kettlewell claims, this process is like undergoing surgery without anesthetics. But we can all learn that feelings will not kill us, that it's okay to experience hurtful emotions, and that we do not have to act (either immediately or eventually) on our emotions. The book of Psalms invites people to feel pain without immediate resolution. At the same time, it encourages stalwart hope in an all-sufficient God:

> Weeping may go on all night,
> > but joy comes with the morning. (30:5)

Identifying and ultimately analyzing our emotions also allow us to experience freedom from the distorted beliefs that precipitate and perpetuate our broken behaviors. During my own counseling and journey of healing, my therapist, Donya Duggleby, asked me to look at these words, found in Matthew 5:4: "Blessed are those who mourn, for they will be comforted" (NRSV). She asked me what they meant. I gave the standard answer, perhaps a bit cynically: "God will comfort me in this hard time." Gently she probed, "What else do you see?" At the time, I was mired in the pain of postpartum depression. I mourned the loss of my hopes for motherhood and grieved my flagging faith. So I couldn't see anything else. She told me, without piety or judgment, "Jerusha, you have to go through the mourning to find the comfort." If we will endure the night of weeping, if we will mourn, if we will listen to our pain and confront the beliefs behind it, we will ultimately know the Creator of joy and help others know Him too.

Avoiding Oversimplification and Trivialization

Popular psychologists on TV and radio often use simplistic, moralistic aphorisms to reveal why people engage in unhealthy patterns and to "encourage" them to end destructive relationships, assert themselves, and live independently. While these motivational phrases and explanations for people's behavior seem logical and sometimes even "right," there are no easy answers for the questions of self-injury. Making a simplistic link such as, "Oh, you were abused as a child, so you are hurting yourself now" does a disservice to the deep pain and complexity of a person's experience. Deciding that someone's behavior is "not that bad" when compared with others' trivializes the anguish that drives self-inflicted violence. Though it may make us feel safer and more able to face difficulties, this is a false reality. Simplification and trivialization ultimately help no one.

Using Knowledge Appropriately

Of course it's essential to know about self-injury. But abusing information is another story. Trying to force people to stop harming themselves by lobbing intellectual grenades at them does not encourage the kind of emotionally safe and vulnerable relationships that most often help self-injurious individuals.

Using Faith as a Blessing Rather Than a Weapon

In a similar way, overscripturalizing or spiritualizing people's struggles or their paths toward recovery usually arrests rather than encourages recovery. Emphasizing outward behavior rather than the attitude of the heart, for instance, holds many self-injurers hostage. They feel trapped and inadequate within a system of rigid judgment that views being "good" as God's foremost desire. In environments like these, wounded people feel unsafe expressing, let alone feeling, their problems and sorrows. Jesus Christ, however, portrays Himself as concerned not merely with our behaviors but with our experiences and emotions as well. A person of faith who struggles with self-harm (or anger, depression, and so on) will not heal based on spiritualized reprimands: "Well, your problem is that you don't have enough faith [or don't pray enough or don't read the Bible enough]!" or "All you need to do is forgive the person who hurt you!" As we learn to differentiate between the bad things we've done and the painful things we've experienced, we can help others do so as well. Not every problem can be solved simply through prayer and confession. Sin needs to be addressed, surely, but wounded feelings also need healing.

Rejecting Shame-Ridden and Guilt-Tripping Messages

Some parents feel tempted to punish self-harming children. They may, for instance, take away privileges after an episode of self-inflicted violence. Some counselors threaten to terminate therapy if a person harms himself or herself. Other loved ones try to motivate behavior change with statements such as, "Don't you see what this is doing to us?," "Don't you want to get better?," or "Can't you see that God doesn't want you to do this?" But turning up the guilt and shame of self-injury does not work in the way people hope it will. Instead, it affirms the devastating messages that self-harmers often live with already: "I'm bad," "I can't really change," or "I don't deserve any better than this." We can refuse to use shaming and guilt-tripping messages. Instead, we can acknowledge that self-injurers are doing the best they presently can to deal with emotional pain. We can trust that with time and help, as they are enabled, they can learn to cope in healthier ways. Shame and guilt will not help them get there.

Steering Clear of Threatening, Demanding, and Trying to Convince Self-Injurers That Their Behavior Is Unreasonable

People are rarely motivated by threats. Demands may initially produce more acceptable behavior, but without authentic heart transformation, threats fail to accomplish lasting change. This proves especially true when a person feels unable to control his or her actions (and this is often the case with self-harmers). Breaking the pattern of self-inflicted violence solely at the insistence of another person almost always ends in disappointment and failure on both sides. Instead of demanding, threatening, or trying to convince self-harmers that their behavior is unreasonable, lean in and listen to the deep meaning they affix to their self-inflicted violence. If you will take the time to uncover why self-harm seems to makes sense for the person you love, you will be better equipped to help over the long haul.

Watching Out for Hypocrisy

Self-injurers often report that they continually received confusing, inconsistent, and sometimes hypocritical messages while growing up (at home, church, school, and so forth). In rigid, dogmatic environments, sensitive individuals struggle watching people declare one thing and live another. Those who express "deep faith" may behave in ways antithetical to the teachings of the church they espouse devotion to. And abusive family members may bestow praise on and claim love for the very relatives they later injure. Part of coming alongside a self-harmer who grew up with double messages will include modeling consistency and authenticity in your own life. Working with teenagers for a decade, I've witnessed their keen eye for a "fake." They often sense nuance, ambiguity, discrepancy between word and action, and inauthentic emotion better than adults do. Self-wounders tend to retain this powerful ability beyond their teenage years. If you are telling self-harmers to face their pain and learn to communicate but aren't doing so yourself, you will lose their respect and your position as an influencer in their lives. More important, self-injurers can tell if you *really* care. If you don't, they will tune you out. A good rule of thumb can be summed up in this oft-used phrase: "People don't care what you know until they know that you care."

Learning to Empathize Rather Than Sympathize

Empathy allows you to enter the emotional world of another person. Sympathy, on the other hand, often makes people the objects of pity. This apparent condescension can alienate people who turn to us for understanding and help. In an effort to encourage empathy, one therapist urges those close to a self-wounder to spend a full day with red streaks drawn on their arms. Making the marks look as much like self-inflicted cuts as possible heightens the experience of shame, disconnection from others, and emotional distress that self-injurers commonly feel. Whether or not you try an exercise like this, empathetically getting inside the world of any wounded person will help you better understand and love him or her. (It's important to consider whether the self-harmer you know would feel encouraged or offended because you chose to try this sort of experiment, so use caution and discernment with it. If you have a strong relationship, you might want to ask the person you're trying to empathize with. If your relationship is strained, it's probably best to ask someone else or hold off on trying something along these lines.)

Helping the Self-Harmer Create an Environment
Conducive to Recovery

As much as we might like to, none of us can create a *completely* safe environment for those we love. Getting rid of every potentially dangerous object is next to impossible and ultimately ineffective anyway. Creating a "clean" environment only perpetuates the illusion that external conditions can determine someone's well-being. Lasting transformation comes only as the mind, not the number of harmful objects in the house, changes. In *The Scarred Soul*, Dr. Tracy Alderman relates the story of a woman recovering from her self-wounding behaviors. During therapy, Dr. Alderman suggested Jackie change her surroundings to make them less compatible with cutting. Though she could not bring herself to trash the razor blades she had used, Jackie found that she *could* lock them in a box in the back of her closet. Eventually, she could throw away the key. If she wanted to harm herself, she could not access the blades, which meant she had to leave her house to get more.[2] Dr. Alderman did not make Jackie's environment safe. But her counsel did help Jackie pursue a home situation more conducive to healthy behavior and recovery.

Doing What You Can

When a person is hurting, it's sometimes overwhelming to be asked, "What can I do to help?" The person you love may not be able to imagine anything that will bring relief. Perhaps you could make suggestions instead. Offer to give your loved one a ride to the doctor or therapist. Waiting with him or her during the appointment may help. Most self-injurers struggle with being alone too much, so being present with the self-injurer is a huge ministry in itself. Asking (nonjudgmentally) if you can help with dishes, laundry, or other housework may encourage a self-harmer. Practicing spontaneous acts of kindness (for instance, "I know you love [fill in the blank] so I picked some up for you") may significantly lift a person's flagging spirits. And providing a distraction for a self-injurer who feels particularly vulnerable can work wonders. Going for a walk or out to a movie, for example, won't erase negative thoughts or feelings, but sometimes a distraction relieves anxiety enough to get beyond the most intense part of the battle. You may feel guilty trying to distract a person from uncomfortable emotions. Isn't facing pain one of the major parts of recovery? Absolutely. But diverting a person's energy and focus for a short time is *not* the same as telling the person to stuff or ignore his or her feelings. It's merely injecting something life-building (time spent together) into a potentially life-devastating situation. During therapy or when the powerful urge to self-harm passes is a better time to confront difficult emotions. In appendix C you will find an extensive list of other activities you can suggest a self-injurer do alone or with you.

Showing Your Faithful Commitment

Many self-harmers live with a life-debilitating fear of abandonment. Some have indeed been rejected by people all their lives. Others perceive—for a wide variety of reasons—that they have been, or will be at any minute, cast aside. That's why it is crucial for loved ones to show they will lovingly stick with a person on the path of recovery. If you fear that you can't make it, that the fight is too fierce, you are in good company. We all feel that at one time or another. And there are probably a number of people reading this book who have been trying to help a self-injurer (or many) for a *long* time. I know that it is exhausting. I know that it feels hopeless sometimes, especially when someone you've been caring for relapses or blatantly rejects help. I know that I've been tempted to give up; I actually have given up before. I felt like I couldn't take it when one girl in our youth group kept inflicting violence on herself despite my and other people's attempts to help her. Thankfully, God's power shows up best when we are weak. It's not just a cliché that He can equip you for the battle. He can bring someone else to come alongside the self-harmer you care about if you cannot take it anymore. Your human limits (even your selfish decisions) cannot doom someone to relapse or failure to recover. Of course it's important to not make promises we won't keep. Be lovingly honest about what you can give. And follow through with what you *are* able to do. God will stretch you, and He will also reveal His faithful strength in your weakness.

WHAT YOU CAN MODEL FOR THE SELF-INJURER

Recovery from anything requires relearning: reframing misguided thoughts and unhealthy patterns of behavior. Loved ones like you can help model for self-harmers the following truth-based and grace-filled thought patterns and behaviors.

Living in Healthy Self-Perception

Do you know your own worth? Who determines whether you are valuable or lovable? Are you confident in and content with who you have been created to be? For many of us, these have been (or are) difficult questions to answer. The self-injurers you care about very likely battle an inaccurate and self-deprecating view of themselves.

As many of us know, the Bible is full of words that declare the incredible value God places on *every* person. But remember, no verse or spiritual truth will magically end a self-injurer's pain. Perhaps using simple, less direct examples like the following will help slowly introduce a self-harmer to the concept of healthy self-perception:

There are two ways to determine worth. A creator can affix value to that which he fashions. If I sculpted a vase, I would have the right to value it at, say, $6,000. In this sense, I — creator of said piece of pottery — have determined the vase's worth. Or, one could also ascertain a thing's value by finding out how much someone else is willing to pay for it. God used both of these methods when He created you and when He affirms your worth. And He talks about it again and again in the form of His creation and the death of Jesus, among many other examples in the Bible.

The self-harmers you care about may or may not be interested in talking about these ideas at greater length. If they are, you can help illuminate the truth that they are incomparably valuable. If they don't want to go further (or if they clearly reject this idea), don't push it. You can trust that the truth will influence them in the time and way it should.

One more thing before we move on: If you do not have a strong sense of your own self-worth, it may be difficult for you to truly help the people you love see that *they* are valuable. Of course, none of us has a perfectly healthy self-image, but even demonstrating a search for authentic and lasting personal value can cause the self-harmer you care about to take note. As you live out the confidence of your own immense worth more and more, you will help others do so as well.

Using Appropriate Communication Skills

This requires asking yourself more tough questions: Do you process your feelings before speaking? Do you assume responsibility for the way your communication style and behaviors affect others? Do you deal with loved ones in a considerate (nonshaming, life-affirming) manner? Do you recognize when you are wrong? Can you discern when another person should responsibly own up to his or her behavior? Are you able to express and do you honestly articulate your needs and desires to loved ones?

Sociologists and psychologists divide communication into two categories: instrumental and affective. The exchange of factual information comprises the instrumental class. Affective communication includes the emotions connected with stories and experiences and the way people understand and process what happens to or around them. Some people, self-wounders included, communicate well on an instrumental level. For many self-injurers, however, an affective language for emotion—especially for pain—has never been formed. How do children who grow up thinking that bad news and personal problems are strictly "off-limits" learn to articulate their hurts, frustrations, and fears? How do those who have never witnessed affective communication express their deep needs? Many self-wound.

Caroline Kettlewell chronicles the way deficient communication skills contributed to her twenty years of self-harm. She writes,

> My family . . . had so profoundly lost the language . . . for the awkward and the uncomfortable and the unpleasant that we didn't even know something was missing. It's not that we lived in a strained silence. . . . To the contrary, we went for words in a big way . . . [but] there was something out there, something you couldn't dare to acknowledge: a writhing Pandora's box of frustrations determinedly quashed, angry words bitten back, sorrows unvoiced. It could bring down the world if opened. . . . No one would ever be so presumptuous as to ask about your troubles, and you would never be so presumptuous as to tell.[3]

You may think that because you're talking about your day or what went on at work, you are communicating with those around you. And you are. But are you processing emotion? Are you getting beyond the facts? Like Ms. Kettlewell, many self-injurers grow up in homes that lack a language for pain, risk, and sorrow. They use blood and burns to scream what they cannot say or have not been taught to say.

The more we grow and mature into effective communicators, the more we can help those who cannot express themselves well. People can learn healthy, affective communication only by watching and imitating it. If they see only disconnected, distant relationships in the world around them, if they never develop a language for their hurt, how can we expect anything but unprocessed pain, deficient relational skills, and self-destructive behaviors? Modeling how, when, and why to articulate feelings is an invaluable gift.

Dealing with Life Patiently

In his excellent course on spiritual direction, *Tell It Slant*, Eugene Peterson claims that working with addicts revealed a fascinating reality to him: One of the primary skills substance abusers need to learn is how to live when *not* in crisis. The same is true of many self-injurers. They become accustomed to moving from one crisis of feeling or circumstance to another. You can model how to patiently deal with the difficulties of life. Showing grace under fire will help a self-harmer immensely. For instance, poor performance at work or school sends many self-wounders into a frenzied state of self-condemnation. This often leads to cutting, burning, and other forms of self-injury. As you humbly discuss the problematic situations in your own life and how you worked to face them with faith and trust, you will help the self-harmer you love practice living without crisis.

Choosing When to Relinquish or Exert Control

We all are well aware that life hands us things we can and can't control. And the things we can't control *significantly* outnumber those we can. In life, there are times to negotiate, times to stand firm, and times to let go. We can help self-injurers by releasing the illusion that we have total control and helping them to do so as well.

Establishing and Maintaining Healthy Boundaries

An important area of personal choice is establishing and maintaining boundaries. Setting limits with ourselves and others is a crucial part of maturity and healing. Emotionally, boundaries give us the freedom to handle our own feelings and separate ourselves from the unhealthy emotions of others. Boundaries also ensure that our own thoughts and dreams are distinct from and as valuable as those of others. With our mind and body, we draw physical boundaries: who can touch us, when, why, and how. Many self-injurers never learn how to set limits with others or themselves. You can model how to do this. Start by encouraging the self-harmer to establish boundaries with "safe" people (like you). Encourage this person that it's okay to want to go where he or she desires for dinner or express an idea that differs from yours. Even seemingly small steps like these are important ones, ones that will encourage further growth in the establishment and upholding of personal limits. You can also help a self-injurer grow by maintaining your own boundaries. For instance, you can lovingly communicate the truth that you cannot be a perfect, or the only, source of support and guidance for your loved one, thereby displaying a healthy and realistic approach to personal limits. You can also set time limits on phone calls, visits, or even details of stories told, depending, of course, on the context of your relationship.

There may very well be times when self-harmers push (or completely overstep) your boundaries. This provides another opportunity for you to discuss openly and honestly why limits are important. You can communicate that in order to be a friend/mentor/helper to people you love, you need time and space to refuel and refresh. You can graciously and firmly ask that they respect your limits. True, this could potentially hurt the feelings of self-injurers you care about. They may feel angry or rejected. But you are not responsible for their reactions or their behaviors, even if they end up inflicting violence on themselves. Faithfully maintaining your boundaries, even when the self-harmers you care about need help to understand why or don't understand at all, will be of great benefit to them.

Practicing Emotional Sobriety

I grew up in a *very* dramatic household. Intense love and fierce anger existed in close quarters. For years and years, I believed that weeping or yelling were the best ways to relieve painful emotions. As I learned (and continue to learn) how to appropriately process, express, and relieve my rage and heartache, however, I realized that I could teach—both explicitly and by example—my own children, the students in our youth group, and the people around me to do so as well. Living an emotionally sober life does *not* mean that feelings are rigidly controlled, that anger is stuffed, that squealing with delight is unhealthy, that tears are forbidden. Rather, emotional sobriety involves processing emotions in ways appropriate to the situation at hand.

Giving and Receiving Appropriate Physical Touch

Self-injury is a profoundly *physical* act. And self-harmers often report a lack of physical touch in their homes and relationships. Self-inflicted violence may be a cry for affectionate touch and nurturing.

Learning how to lovingly give and receive physical affection can be a significant step in the self-wounder's recovery, especially if he or she has never known how to before. Family members and other loved ones surrounding the self-harmer can help in this process by modeling and offering healthy touch.

Recognizing the Importance of Spiritual Healing

Because of the complex nature of this particular issue, we've devoted an entire forthcoming chapter to the subject. For now, keep in mind that recovery is not complete without the spiritual healing that brings mental and physical restoration to the fullest realization.

You've taken in a lot over the last few pages. Processing what you've learned may require much thought and time, and it will certainly take some time to implement any suggestions you've found helpful into your own life. When you find that you're frustrated or confused, take a couple of steps back and regroup. And as you walk alongside the self-wounders in your life, take heart: What you are doing *matters*. You are making a difference.

7 DRESSING THE WOUNDS
METHODS OF TREATMENT AND WHY THEY MATTER

─────────── IN MY EXPERIENCE ───────────

BY DR. EARL HENSLIN

Ed came to my office for help with depression and anxiety shortly after his twenty-ninth birthday. A fifteen-inch walking cast covered most of his left leg. During the intake evaluation, I discovered that Ed's girlfriend of four years had recently ended their relationship, telling Ed that she could no longer deal with his obsessions and compulsions. He spiraled into the despairing, nervous state I found him in shortly thereafter.

Ed self-injured, but never through the more common forms of cutting and burning. Instead, Ed impulsively, self-destructively exercised. The stress fracture in Ed's left leg, the one that necessitated his long walking cast, had been the result of excessive, strenuous running.

Ed's MD strongly suggested that he refrain from working out for thirty days. But Ed discovered that when he ran, even though excruciating pain coursed through his foot and leg, he felt better emotionally. Only when the physical ache was severe enough could Ed concentrate on that pain and stop obsessing about whether his girlfriend would have dropped him if only he had done this or that.

Self-injurious exercise had become a comfort and pain reliever for Ed. Over time, however, just like any addiction, it took longer and more intense exercise to get the same emotional relief.

It would have been easy to focus our therapy on Ed's current troubles, especially on the breakup of his long-term relationship and the potential, irreversible damage Ed could wreak on his body. But working with a

SPECT scan and EMDR (a treatment option we will discuss later in this chapter), as well as within the framework of traditional "talk" therapy, I discovered other, deeper sources of emotional distress that compelled Ed to wound his body again and again.

As we processed the reasons behind Ed's self-injury, grievous memories from young adulthood came to light. During Ed's adolescence, his mom had an affair and ultimately left his father—and her children—for another man. Ed had absolutely no contact with his mother for over a year.

The ache of being abandoned at sixteen years old came pouring out. Deep inside, Ed felt his mother's infidelity and neglect were punishments from God. When Ed's girlfriend left, it triggered the old, unhealed pain of his mother's affair. He literally tried to run away from his emotional hurts but found that no matter how strenuous and agonizing the exercise, the heartache would come back a short while later, each time with a much stronger force.

Helping Ed recognize the connection between his self-injurious behaviors and the brokenness of his relationships became a significant part of his therapy. Ultimately, through addressing Ed's physical and familial traumas and integrating medical and psychological methods, Ed began the journey of healing that freed him to be the man God created him to be.

WHEN OUR ROLE IS LIMITED

Ed's story confirms that nonprofessionals (like most of us) can do a lot, but we can't do everything. We just spent an entire chapter looking at the many ways we can encourage healing, but the self-injurers in our lives will likely need the help of trained clinicians (therapists, doctors, and the like) as well. Qualified practitioners can administer help to those we care about in ways that most of us cannot.

Within many communities and churches, lay counselors (who are unlicensed but trained), volunteers, and mentors work with people battling issues like self-harm. In the youth group in which I serve, all leaders receive some instruction on how to help young people work through the difficulties they face. The key in this equation is that lay counselors, mentors, and volunteers have been equipped through training.

But even with some education, laypeople often want and need to work in conjunction with professionals. It's best to carefully evaluate what you and other unlicensed people can do.

Many—actually most—self-harmers will benefit from the assistance of a professional therapist. But therapy is not limited to the methods with which many of us are familiar. In fact, over the next few pages, we will discuss many therapeutic paths to recovery, beginning with more common modes of therapeutic treatment and continuing with less traditional methods. Some may be familiar to you; others may initially strike you as strange.

You may be concerned because of financial worries. Perhaps you've wanted to get the self-injurer you care about connected with a doctor or counselor, but you wonder how in the world people can afford expensive treatments like therapy and brain scanning.

It may take some time and effort, but you can help the self-wounder you love find ways to provide for the help he or she needs. Most lay counseling is free or can be if financial need is demonstrated. Many professional therapists work on sliding scales and with insurance companies.

Your church or community may offer no-obligation grants for medical or psychotherapeutic help. The National Coalition of Mental Health Professionals and Consumers, Inc., can also assist you (look for information on this organization later in this chapter). And research facilities or universities that often have access to the latest technology and treatment options can help as well.

I realize that it may be hard for you or the self-harmer you love to ask for help, especially from strangers. But be encouraged: The benefits of effective treatment will be *well worth* any effort you exert or humbling you experience.

Please look at all these forms of treatment with an open mind. The method you least understand or the one you worry you could never afford could be the very one that would best help a self-harmer you love.

INDIVIDUAL THERAPY

The form of therapy you may be best acquainted with is called psychotherapy or "talk" therapy. People make an appointment, see a counselor,
and discuss what's going on or what went on in their life. Primarily,
clients see their therapist alone; on occasion, they may invite a family
member or friend to join them for special sessions.

Within the broad category of individual therapy, there are several distinct approaches a counselor may take. *Psychodynamic* therapy
focuses on what prompts behavior and why a person feels compelled to
act in a certain way. *Cognitive-behavioral* therapy assumes that a person's thought life powerfully influences how he or she lives and feels.
Supportive therapy helps patients manage the day-in, day-out business
of life. *Faith-based* counseling focuses on the spiritual dimensions of
behavior and the motivations behind it. And this is by no means an
exhaustive list of the clinical forms of therapy.

I believe the most effective counseling combines elements of all of
these approaches. I trust that in reading about the role of experience
and brain chemistry in self-inflicted violence, you've seen that the mind,
body, and soul are intimately connected. Consequently, in order to facilitate genuine healing, therapy should address the internal dialogues and
cognitive distortions (the toxic beliefs that precipitate unhealthy actions)
of the mind. It should help with the physical, daily realities of life. And
it should always care for the wounded spirit.

Psychotherapy is not a magic cure for self-injury. And it's certainly
not a "quick fix." It often takes significant amounts of time, money, and
effort to unravel the faulty coping mechanism of self-harm.

In fact, during the initial stages of individual therapy, people often
feel worse before they feel better. As they confront difficult emotions
and memories, they feel threatened. They have lost the "anesthetic" (self-
injury) they used to dull pain; it feels unbearable. Indeed, many stop
therapy before it really starts to help.

But I believe therapy is almost always crucial to a self-harmer's journey toward recovery. Self-inflicted violence is a serious problem that

cannot be solved solely by sympathetic (even empathetic) love and support. A trained professional—whether you choose a psychiatrist, psychotherapist, or both—can help self-harmers process their experiences in an objective, calm way—a way that loved ones invested in the individual and inadvertently biased by their own beliefs cannot.

So if therapy is so important, what exactly can it do? What can it *not* do? Let's look first at the benefits of therapy.

It helps people identify and express their feelings.

Many self-harmers cannot even acknowledge that they are in pain or that their behavior is destructive. As we've mentioned again and again, they often feel their pain is too overwhelming to face. The consistent presence of a "safe" person, a person who can objectively encourage self-injurers to express themselves, is invaluable.

It helps individuals develop practical skills.

In therapy, self-injurers can learn to cope with pain by thinking and talking rather than wounding. For most people, life is so stressful that it's impossible to make it without some method of soothing the self. If people don't have body- and soul-nourishing ways to manage stress, such as exercise, reading, hobbies, or prayer, they will turn to destructive ways, such as sexual promiscuity, drinking, drugs, or self-injury. Therapy teaches people how to use positive internal and external resources to manage the inevitable stresses of life.

It sets aside time and energy for healing.

Dr. Henslin rightly observes that recovery is *not* accidental. It involves a deliberate examination of the past and present, as well as a concerted effort to break destructive patterns and reframe harmful thoughts. If time and energy are not specifically devoted to recovery, it simply won't happen. Committing to regular counseling provides the space and time to focus on healing. It also gives those who feel guilty when talking about themselves the "excuse" to do so.

It provides space and limits for self-examination.

In order to live a full and whole life, people must carefully evaluate their beliefs, behaviors, and emotions. But we cannot live in a perpetual state of introspection, and self-harmers can easily fall into narcissistic thinking. Therapy provides needed space for self-examination, but limits it as well. Of course, people will most likely need to process what's happening in therapy between sessions too.

It helps reframe a broken reality.

Self-harmers often struggle to understand the world around them. Their perceptions have been skewed and fragmented by the painful experiences of their past or present. A therapist can help individuals reorient their vision and establish a healthier way to interact with others.

Therapy has its limits, however. It's important to recognize that counseling is not a "cure-all." Here are some things therapy *cannot* do.

It cannot replace the emotional support and love you
and others have to offer.

Clinicians may care about their patients, even a great deal. But they cannot develop the same kind of loving relationship with self-injurers that family, friends, pastors, and other loved ones can.

Though it may be tempting to do so, we cannot assume that once self-wounders find a counselor, they don't need us anymore. In reality, as they work through painful memories and experiences, they may need us more than ever. In addition, you may feel jealous once your self-harming loved one begins to develop a relationship with his or her counselor and shares with you details of their interactions. But we don't have to leave the people who hurt themselves, the people we care about, strictly in a professional's hands. It is especially important that we keep our loving support close during the difficult work of therapy.

It cannot force someone to get better.

Self-harmers may enter therapy with a hard heart. They may seem to know it all, able to spout off psychological terms and reasons for their behavior. They may be willing to talk all around their issues but won't venture into the territory of the heart. Or they may deflect every question with an irrelevant comment. On the other extreme, some self-injurers have "nothing to say." Perhaps they don't want to face their own weakness or acknowledge that they, or others, are flawed. Maybe they fear that experiencing feelings will be too dangerous, so it's best not to start at all. Of course, since many self-injurers struggle with communication, there's the possibility that the therapist is working with someone who literally has no language to express his or her emotions. The bottom line is that therapy cannot force anyone to genuinely open up and heal. Even gaining insight ("knowing it all") will not eradicate pain or even alleviate symptoms. Only authentic heart engagement with therapy will encourage recovery. And though we cannot control another person's motivation or his or her commitment to healing, we can certainly pray that the self-wounder we care about will vulnerably submit to the work of therapy.

It cannot prevent relapse.

People who start therapy may not immediately stop self-injuring. In fact, as they begin to evaluate their emotions and experiences, self-harmers may initially feel even stronger urges to hurt themselves. It's best, actually, to anticipate that setbacks will happen because we will then be better equipped to face them. People may relapse by returning to self-injurious patterns, tampering with their medication, failing to comply with the counsel they are given, or overtly refusing help. But don't be wholly discouraged. A setback does not mean that you're back at square one. Sustained by grace and strength, pick up where you are.

It cannot provide instant results.

The first few sessions of therapy often focus on establishing a person's history. There's a lot of factual interchange between counselor and counselee. Some people feel concerned, even angry: "Sitting here talking about my childhood isn't going to help. I want to know what I can do when I go home and want to slice up my arm." If we can be patient and encourage self-harmers to be patient, we can help them stay committed for the long haul.

It cannot protect people from bad counsel.

Unfortunately, obtaining a license to practice psychotherapy or achieving a doctorate in psychology does not ensure that a person will provide effective and caring advice. Bad therapy is a reality.

A friend of mind realized only after some time that instead of helping her overcome the issues in her life, the professional counselor she had been seeing was creating an unhealthy dependence on him and on therapy. He suggested she come in for more and more sessions until she felt as though she couldn't face the day without his advice. Finally, she recognized the pattern and severed the relationship. This woman persevered with the work of recovery despite this horrific experience and found an excellent counselor who has helped her greatly on her journey to wholeness.

I know others who had a bad experience with counseling and have written off the whole idea. Although it's completely understandable why someone would write off therapy after an especially bad experience with it, it is unrealistic and unproductive to do so. You may try to help skeptical self-injurers you know work though this by using an example of eating out (or something like this): If they visited one bad restaurant, would they refuse to eat out for the rest of their lives? Spending time and money on bad therapy is, of course, much more frustrating and disheartening than having a bad meal. It can be a devastating blow to entrust the one you care for to a person who misuses the position of authority he or she has been given.

But I give you this encouragement: For every one bad therapist, there are *many* caring and consistent ones who chose their field because they genuinely want to serve and help people. Even if the person you love initially starts with a poor counselor, he or she does not have to continue, but instead can move on and find someone who will use this powerful and important tool appropriately and compassionately.

It cannot change life itself.

Counseling helps people reframe their thoughts, evaluate their beliefs and behaviors, and better engage with the world. But it does not take the challenges, conflicts, and painful experiences out of life. It cannot erase the memories of a wounded past. It will not permanently change people's emotional makeup. They may still be prone to extreme emotions or imbalanced chemistry. Therapy *can* help people learn to cope with life, but it cannot transform it.

GROUP THERAPY

Group therapy may be structured, unstructured, issue focused, mixed, family based, or a combination of some or all of these. And while group therapy is superintended by a licensed professional, the level of his or her involvement will differ from group to group.

Generally speaking, the greater the number of genuinely committed people involved in therapy and recovery, the more powerful treatment becomes. Building a network of people who support and participate with a self-injurer in therapy can promote the recovery process significantly.

Over the next few paragraphs, I'd like to describe several forms of group therapy for you, as well as highlight some of their potential strengths and weaknesses.

In a *structured group*, individuals come together and proceed through a series of exercises and lessons geared toward helping them process and change their unhealthy patterns.

Unstructured groups focus more on conversation. Members relate to one another, offering support and the chance to learn and practice effective communication skills.

Issue-focused groups bring people with similar problems together. In the case of self-inflicted violence, a group would include self-harmers of different types. Those who cut, burn, or engage in self-injurious exercise or eating patterns may be grouped together.

Mixed groups include people of differing experience and struggle. In a mixed group, people learn how to interact with others who see the world differently than they do. They can "get outside their world" by listening to the experiences of others. But they may feel misunderstood by others in the group or isolated because of their particular battle.

Family-based therapy helps relatives locked in dysfunctional patterns break free and develop skills everyone can benefit from, such as healthy communication, coping mechanisms, and methods of self-evaluation. During family therapy, a therapist may ask relatives to reenact a negative situation that could or did occur at home. For instance, a father and son who have difficulty communicating may discuss a volatile topic on which they disagree. As an objective observer, the therapist can help them see the helpful and harmful things that were said and done.

Within family therapy, there's another form of group therapy that brings together several families working toward healing and wholeness. These *multifamily groups* help individuals observe positive and negative patterns in other families facing similar situations. Multifamily groups allow parents, siblings, and spouses who feel isolated to connect with others in situations like theirs. They may feel relieved to know their loved one is not the only one making destructive choices and can grow from listening to and watching other people. But what comes out in family counseling can become destructive if members leverage what was said or done against each other. Using therapy as a club to beat one another over the head ("You're not supposed to do that! Don't you remember what Doctor _____ said?") does not promote healthy change or trust building.

Again, there are strengths and weaknesses to each of these forms of group therapy. Structured groups may be too rigid for some. Unstructured groups may be too free-flowing for others.

Some people may feel that the ideas and experiences expressed in group therapy are redundant. But even this has a positive side. It has been said that the average human needs to hear something about seven times for it to fully sink in. Consistently revisiting the basics may actually prove an important aspect of recovery.

And according to the research of Dr. Irvin D. Yalom, Professor Emeritus of Psychiatry at the Stanford University School of Medicine and author of *The Theory and Practice of Group Psychotherapy*, individuals almost always benefit from the emotional catharsis, interpersonal relationships, and mutually supportive learning of group therapy. Members also experience the self-affirming reality that they can help others. Group therapy may be a powerful aid in the healing process of self-wounders you care about.

It is important, however, to recognize that groups—particularly issue-focused groups—can dissolve into a place where individuals share "war stories" rather than pursue genuine healing. Graphically discussing self-injury can even become a substitute for the act itself. A good facilitator can steer members away from this damaging aspect of group therapy, so be certain to evaluate or interview the supervising therapist before deciding on a group. (You'll find more suggestions for choosing a therapist in appendix A.)

Finally, in order to maximize the benefits of any group, it's also important to assess the dynamics of the group (structured or unstructured) and the personality of prospective participants (reserved or outgoing).

MUTUAL-HELP GROUPS

Over forty years ago, two brave men established Alcoholics Anonymous. Most mutual-help groups, including Christian ones like Celebrate Recovery and Overcomers Outreach, use principles similar to the twelve steps first laid out in AA.

Because mutual-help groups like AA are structured in such a way that no supervising clinician oversees meetings, they are not considered group therapy or a form of medical treatment. Instead, leaders and sponsors are individuals who have worked through the program, experienced some time in sobriety, and made themselves available to help others.

Therapists and psychiatrists often encourage participation in a mutual-help group as an adjunct to counseling. These gatherings provide another form of consistent support, another place to develop healthy relational and communication skills, and a "safe" place to go.

Sadly, Christians sometimes avoid mutual-help groups because of ideas such as this: "Jesus is the only support I need. If I share my problems with Him, everything will work out." It's true: Jesus *is* enough for you. He *is* always there for you and *will* minister to you in the direst circumstances. But He has created us to experience His love and healing through relationship with others. No one experiences healing in isolation. We feel His embrace in the hugs people give us. We experience His grace and compassion through phone calls, notes, and support during tough times. Recovery takes place in the everyday world of relationship.

OTHER LESS COMMON FORMS OF TREATMENT

Dialectical Behavior Therapy (DBT)

Although Dialectical Behavior Therapy is not as readily available as traditional individual therapy, it has proved an extremely effective means of treating borderline personality disorder and self-injurious behaviors of all kinds (including eating disorders).

Developed by psychologist Dr. Marsha Linehan of the University of Washington in Seattle, DBT integrates acceptance (you can embrace where you are today) and change (you can do better) and combines these two forces to form the fundamental "dialectic"—loosely defined as weighing and assimilating contradictory ideas with the goal of resolution—that drives this method of treatment.

DBT recognizes the difficulty in treating self-harming patients who often feel "put off by [traditional therapy's] constant focus on change." During clinical research, Linehan found that "as acceptance strategies were added to the change strategies, clients felt their therapists understood them much better. They stayed in treatment instead of dropping out . . . and improved faster."[1]

Engaging in Dialectical Behavior Therapy involves a significant time commitment from both client and therapist, as it incorporates both "skills group and individual therapy. . . . Skills of emotion regulation, mindfulness, interpersonal effectiveness, and distress tolerance are taught in group once a week. Individual therapy, once a week, is the opportunity to check with a therapist regarding the week's practice of skills learned in group."[2] Weekly telephone contact with the individual therapist is another component of DBT.

Theophostic Prayer Ministry (TPM)

Christians reading this book may have heard about an increasingly popular form of treatment known as theophostic counseling, theophostic therapy, or, most appropriately, Theophostic Prayer Ministry (this is not only what founder Ed Smith calls it, but it's also the most appropriately descriptive term for the practice).

In fact, according to Elliot Miller's evaluation of TPM for the *Christian Research Journal*, Theophostic Prayer Ministry is spreading more quickly in evangelical circles than almost any other approach to inner healing.[3] TPM is also highly controversial, provoking zealous pro or con pronouncements from supporters and critics.

TPM takes its name from two Greek words that, when combined, mean "the light of God." The Theophostic Prayer Ministries website, www.theophostic.com, explains its exclusively Christian approach: TPM is

> Christ centered and God reliant for its direction and
> outcome. . . . Simply stated, it is encouraging a person to

discover and expose what he believes that is falsehood and then encouraging him to have an encounter with Jesus Christ through prayer and allowing the Lord to reveal His truth to the wounded person's heart and mind. It is not about advice giving, diagnosing problems, sharing opinions or insight. It is about allowing a person to have a personal encounter with the Lord Jesus in the midst of the person's emotional pain.[4]

So what happens in a typical Theophostic Prayer Ministry session? Elliot Miller explains,

After receiving the recipient's permission to do so, the facilitator invites Jesus into the session and asks Him to reveal His truth about the memories that will be brought to mind. The recipient is then asked to try to identify the memory where she (or he) first felt the emotions that are troubling her in the present (e.g., feeling unloved).[5]

From there, the recipient is encouraged to describe both the circumstances surrounding this memory and how remembering the experience makes her feel ("I'm afraid of being left alone"). The facilitator then asks Jesus to communicate what He wants the recipient to know about the memory and feelings that are distressing her. The recipient waits on Jesus to impress something on her mind—a vision, words, or new insight. This may come in the form of biblical truth ("I will never leave you nor forsake you"), factual truth ("The pain of being deserted as a child is real, but God has given me a loving husband and a supportive network of friends who care about me"), or strong feelings ("I feel ready to forgive the people who abandoned me and will trust that God will not turn His back on me").

The conservative Christian Research Institute (CRI) "finds nothing in TPM's core theory and practice that is inconsistent with Scripture." Still, CRI cautions that there are "specific concerns that Christians could raise regarding TPM's core theory and practice that should not be ignored,"[6] including founder Ed Smith's teachings on spiritual warfare. If you are interested in TPM, the official website is extraordinarily informative. The "What is Theophostic Ministry?" section is especially helpful. A Google search for "Theophostic Prayer Ministry" will yield links to both supporters and critics; I encourage you to research both if you are interested in learning more.

Hospitalization

We can break this form of treatment down into two subcategories: public and private hospitalization.

In the past, medical professionals treated self-harmers as suicidal individuals. If seen in the ER or at a doctor's office, a self-injurer would be readily committed into a long-term psychiatric facility. This is still a relatively common practice.

But more often today, in the era of HMOs and managed care, psychiatric hospitalizations generally last between three days and a week. Public hospitalization now serves more as a means of crisis intervention. Instead of recovery, the primary goals of psychiatric hospitals are to stabilize individuals and return them to the level at which they were functioning before being admitted. Unfortunately, this often results in a revolving-door pattern of hospitalization for repetitive self-injurers. It's not uncommon for a self-harmer to be in and out of hospitals for years. In several accounts I came across, long-term self-injurers had been hospitalized fifty to one hundred times.

Public hospitalizations can, indeed, help stabilize individuals in acute crisis (for instance, people who feel strong suicidal urges or who have severely injured themselves and risk accidental death). But they can also retard the process of recovery. Self-harmers complain that doctors and nurses often—whether directly or indirectly—communicate that they do not deserve as much care as those with accidental injuries.

The same doctors who would do everything possible to save the life of an obese heart-attack victim may refuse anesthesia for stitches, make condescending and shaming remarks, and otherwise treat the self-injurer as an inconvenience. Tragically, this kind of medical "care" may perpetuate a self-harmer's feelings of worthlessness and hopelessness.

Furthermore, public hospitalization has become more and more costly, particularly because many insurance companies require a diagnosis to process claims for treatment. And despite the rising incidence of self-injurious activity and the deep psychological pain that accompanies it, managed-care providers often view self-harmers as chronically untreatable. They may justify withholding funds since deliberate self-harm is not officially recognized in the DSM-IV.

Contrary to public hospital treatment, private hospitalization can be an excellent alternative. Inpatient or outpatient programs can start a person on the journey toward recovery. No one is magically cured at a private hospital, but many learn the basics of how to understand and overcome self-injury there.

The first, and still one of the only, inpatient treatment facilities geared toward self-inflicted violence makes its home at the Linden Oaks Hospital in Edward, Illinois. The S.A.F.E. Alternatives program provides a great example of the benefits of private hospitalization. Combining individual and group therapy, intensive education, guided journaling, and a variety of recreationally therapeutic activities, the S.A.F.E. program is a nationally recognized treatment approach, professional network, and educational resource base. You can find out more at http://www.selfinjury.com/index.html.

Private institutions may offer outpatient treatment as well. Located in Los Angeles, The Healing House runs an intensive outpatient program (IOP). IOPs work well for individuals whose patterns of self-injury interfere with their ability to live day to day. Those who recently have been released from an inpatient facility and those for whom inpatient hospitalization has proved ineffective may benefit from an IOP. Like inpatient programs, IOPs combine therapy, education, and "homework." They are considerably more structured than weekly therapy and can be a valuable alternative to full-time or public hospitaliza-

tion. For more information about The Healing House, see http://www
.thehealinghousela.com/disc2_frm.htm.

Mental-Health Centers in Your Community

Long-term medical treatment, whether in the form of therapy or hospital care, can place significant strain on a family's or individual's
resources. And though it may go against your desire and the way you
were raised, applying for public assistance (including, but not limited
to, welfare) gives you access to the mental-care system in a way your
personal finances may not allow.

Many community health centers take clients in need. You can
find free or low-cost mental-health care through some churches, universities, research facilities, and nonprofit hospitals.

There may even be benefits to working with publicly funded programs. Since state or federally funded hospitals often affiliate themselves with major research and teaching institutions, patients can
benefit from the latest information and treatment methods for minimal cost.

You can inquire with the government offices in your city, county,
and state about sources of funding for mental-health care. You can
also contact the National Coalition of Mental Health Professionals
and Consumers, Inc., in New York (see appendix B for contact
information).

There is no shame in maximizing every available resource for the
one you love (or for yourself). Your life, the life of your loved one, and
the health and stability of your entire family matter most.

Eye Movement Desensitization and Reprocessing (EMDR)

Eye Movement Desensitization and Reprocessing (EMDR) helps individuals access their memories, process and metabolize experiences or
feelings that have been "stuck" in the nervous system, reframe memories and emotions, and ultimately inhibit the revisiting of their trauma-
inducing triggers.[7]

During an EMDR session,

> The therapist works with the client to identify a specific problem as the focus of the treatment session. The client calls to mind the disturbing issue or event, what was seen, felt, heard, thought, etc., and what thoughts and beliefs are currently held about that event. The therapist facilitates the directional movement of the eyes or other dual attention stimulation of the brain, while the client focuses on the disturbing material, and the client just notices whatever comes to mind without making any effort to control direction or content. . . . Sets of eye movements are continued until the memory becomes less disturbing and is associated with positive thoughts and beliefs about one's self.[8]

According to Dr. Ira Dressner, a New York psychotherapist and practitioner certified by the EMDR International Association (EMDRIA), during a typical session, a therapist might facilitate directional movement of the eyes by directing a "client to concentrate on an event or incident while moving their eyes horizontally following the light on an electric screen. Additionally clients wear earphones to hear a soft beep that corresponds to where their eyes are moving. . . . It is not hypnosis neither does it produce any dizziness or headaches."[9]

The EMDRIA website describes in practical terms what happens after a day's therapy:

> Following a successful EMDR session, a person no longer relives the images, sounds, and feelings when the event is brought to mind. You still remember what happened, but it is less upsetting. Many types of therapy have similar goals. However, EMDR appears to be similar to what occurs naturally during dreaming or REM (rapid eye movement) sleep. Therefore, EMDR can be thought of as a physiologically based therapy that helps a person see disturbing material in a new and less distressing way.[10]

According to the EMDRIA, "To date, EMDR has helped an estimated two million people of all ages relieve many types of psychological stress."[11]

Dr. Henslin told me EMDR can be particularly helpful in identifying and debasing triggers for self-harming behavior that stem from trauma such as childhood abuse, abandonment, loss, or exposure to disaster.

If you would like more information, visit the EMDRIA website at www.emdria.org.

Psychological Testing

The idea may seem intimidating, but there's actually nothing mysterious or strange about psychological testing. Conducted for diagnostic purposes, treatment scheduling, and helping professionals make clinical recommendations, psychological tests range from personality questionnaires (such as the MMPI or the Myers-Briggs) to tests that include creative and physical elements, such as drawing, solving puzzles, even building with blocks. Other tests measure memory and cognitive functioning by presenting individuals with math problems or strings of numbers and words to repeat.

Psychological testing may provide excellent information for care providers that you or someone you love are currently seeing. The American Psychological Association gives more information about psychological testing at http://www.apa.org/science/faq-findtests.html. On that same webpage, you can also find practitioners and test administrators in your area.

Biofeedback

According to a profile from the Association for Applied Psychophysiology and Biofeedback,

Biofeedback is a treatment technique in which people are trained to improve their health by using signals from their own bodies. Physical therapists use biofeedback to help stroke victims regain movement in paralyzed muscles. Psychologists use it to help tense and anxious clients learn to relax. Specialists in many different fields use biofeedback to help their patients cope with pain.[12]

Though you probably did not recognize it as such, the last time you took your temperature, you used biofeedback to determine the seriousness of your condition. The thermometer you used "feeds back" information about your body. If you are running a fever, you may decide (and wisely so) to rest and drink plenty of fluids.

Clinicians, in much the same way, rely on complicated biofeedback machines. According to Bette Runck of the National Institute of Mental Health,

> Their machines can detect a person's internal bodily functions with far greater sensitivity and precision than a person can alone. . . . Both patients and therapists use [this information] to gauge and direct the progress of treatment.
>
> For patients, the biofeedback machine acts as a kind of sixth sense which allows them to "see" or "hear" activity inside their bodies. One commonly used type of machine, for example, picks up electrical signals in the muscles. It translates these signals into a form that patients can detect: It triggers a flashing light bulb, perhaps, or activates a beeper every time muscles grow more tense. If patients want to relax tense muscles, they try to slow down the flashing or beeping.[13]

Becoming aware of and able to control the body's responses can prove invaluable for self-injurers, particularly those who feel alienated and disconnected from their own bodies.

Journaling

In Steven Levenkron's experience, "Sometimes writing down thoughts and feelings [is] a less dangerous first step than talking."[14] He recommends that individuals keep a journal (or diary, if you prefer that term) that records feelings, thoughts, and reactions to people and events, as well as self-injurious impulses and actions taken to address them.

Putting emotions and experiences in writing makes them more real. Initially, this can be challenging for self-harmers who would like to distance themselves from, not engage with, pain. But for centuries, writing has been used as a means of cathartic emotional release. The physical act of taking pen to paper (or, perhaps more often in today's day and age, finger to keyboard) also provides tactical stimulation, which many self-wounders crave.

In a journal, self-injurers can vent anger in nonviolent ways. They can confront fears in a safer manner. And they may also discover things they could not have otherwise. Even exploring painful memories may allow them to recall happy times that have been lost in childhood recollections they stuffed under the blanket of self-inflicted violence. Such memories give hope for tomorrow and joy for today.

Like other forms of treatment, journaling has its drawbacks. People sometimes write destructively, repeatedly beating themselves up with words like *fat, ugly, stupid, worthless,* and so on. One way to avoid this pitfall is to encourage self-harmers to share their writing with a trusted person (therapist, pastor, friend, family member) and ask whether he or she agrees or disagrees with the observations expressed. Of course, this may limit a self-injurer's desire or ability to be fully honest, so whether or not sharing the journal is a good idea will ultimately depend on the individual.

Another potential problem comes when a self-wounder feels forced to keep a daily diary. The impulse to write should be encouraged, but rarely do genuinely heartfelt breakthroughs come through commanded journaling. If you want to encourage a self-harmer to write, you may simply offer that if he or she would like to share with you, you are available and interested in what he or she has to say.

Here are some topics that might help a self-wounder process his or her emotions and behaviors:

- How has self-injury changed my body and body image?
- How has self-inflicted violence affected my self-confidence?
- How has self-harm influenced my relationships?
- How has self-injury harmed me spiritually?
- What was my life like before I started self-wounding?
- What do I wish my life was like now?
- What do I like to do?
- What does anger mean to me?
- What does freedom from self-harm mean to me?
- What have I learned while fighting self-injurious impulses?

Of course, there are many other questions that can help people process their behaviors and emotions. I hope these spark some ideas and provide some options for you or for someone you love.

IT'S HARD FOR EVERYONE

Therapy is not easy on anyone. Though it's terrifying for self-harmers to live with self-inflicted violence, it can also be agonizing to live without. Recovery requires surrendering a trusted and at least initially effective coping mechanism. For many, giving self-injury up feels too risky. Indeed, it would be impossible to relinquish self-harm if there were not something far better to trust in.

And I'm not talking about other coping methods. Of course, exercise and meditation and relaxation are wonderful techniques that can promote wholeness. But true healing happens in the presence of, and in surrender to, the One who is faithful and strong and able to save. It's true: Only God can fully restore and redeem the self-injurer's body, mind, and soul.

8 WHEN THE BODY IS RAVAGED, THE SOUL CRIES OUT

EXPLORING THE SPIRITUAL IMPLICATIONS OF SELF-INJURY

I came across a beautiful story of redemption while researching for this book. On SloppyNoodle.com, a young woman who preferred to remain anonymous shared her battle with self-harm in a powerful essay entitled "Only Once."[1]

While sitting in science class, watching time tick by too slowly and listening to an enraged teacher insulting his students and dismissing them as "unruly yobs with no future," this young woman (we'll call her Gretchen) discovered the power of self-injury to drive away uncomfortable emotions.

Picking up a friend's craft knife, Gretchen carved a large Ban the Bomb symbol into her forearm. She writes, "Blood ran everywhere . . . and I felt GOOD. Relieved. Appeased. Justified."

That science class incident sparked seven years of self-injury. And as time went on, self-inflicted violence became Gretchen's "secret friend." She reveals, "I could forget all the pain on the inside if I concentrated on causing pain on the outside. . . . And I truly believed that I deserved to be cut."

Gretchen knew that something was wrong with life and, moreover, wrong with *her*. She was acutely aware that she did bad things, and she assumed that meant she was inherently bad.

Later, Gretchen would note that on the deepest level, "My self-harm was a desperate plea to a God I didn't know." Through self-inflicted wounds, Gretchen cried out, "I know I deserve to die for my sins. Look at my scars! I acknowledge my sin, but I don't want to die!"

The rest of her life hung on these questions: Is there something, some*one*, more powerful than my urge to cut? Is there anything, any*one*, that can wash away the heartache of this world—the pain others have caused me and the wounds I've inflicted on myself?

In the midst of this battle, Gretchen began learning about and drawing near to Jesus. The unnamed God she had been pleading with revealed Himself and reached into her grief-ridden world. He promised to set Gretchen free and heal her scars. She wanted to believe. She needed to believe.

Gretchen writes that after she gave her life to Jesus, she struggled to let go of her need to cut. She says,

> I felt I was letting down the Church, myself and Jesus if I gave way to temptation, but I knew no other way to cope with my feelings. I had been cutting for YEARS. So many wonderful people had told me that I was "justified by the blood of Jesus," but I just could not understand what that meant. I NEEDED to see blood leave my body to know that I was cutting out all the sin, the sadness, the anger, the hatred, the frustration. I cried out to God every day to be set free. Even when I went for several months without cutting, the daily torment and temptation was a cruel and constant reminder of the only coping mechanism I knew.

The battle between condemnation and grace raged fiercely in Gretchen's mind, soul, and body. But late one night, while reading a novel, Gretchen discovered a Truth that allowed her to taste genuine, lasting freedom.

The book Gretchen picked up was *The Book of God* by Walter Wangerin Jr., which tells the story of the Bible in narrative form. When she reached the portion that detailed Christ's crucifixion, she recalls,

> The pain, humiliation and suffering he went through was described so powerfully. It wasn't sensationalised, it wasn't glamorously gruesome . . . it was just really, really REAL. I could hardly bear to read on. MY JESUS! How could this happen to my Jesus? I was wracked with sobbing, reading through tears about the most horrendous suffering of the most wonderful, precious person that had ever lived. "WHY?" I cried out to God. "WHY?" "How could You let this happen? To your Son?!" And the Lord spoke two, gentle words to me. Two words changed my life.
> "ONLY ONCE."

Suddenly, Gretchen understood. She had been spilling her own blood in a desperate attempt to make things right, to show that she was sorry, to prove that she deserved to be hurt, to end the raging pain inside her. But no wound ever bled enough or went deep enough to last. No cut she made would *ever* satisfy the ache within. There would always be another reason to destroy, to punish, to heal herself through cutting.

How clear it was: Jesus lived to bleed—once and for all—for *every* reason she "needed" or "wanted" to cut. She was right all along: Blood *did* atone. But her blood was insufficient, so He bled in her place. He had suffered *all* of her shame and offered her the freedom to lay down her self-injury forever.

Of course, God works in each of our lives differently, so one person's experience with healing may not—probably *will* not—look the same as another's. Every self-injurer who seeks God will experience something unique—His truth will be just what that person needs. But for Gretchen, the words "only once" finally ended her grueling battle with self-injury. She never needed to bleed again.

INSIDE A CUTTER'S MIND

A MOMENT AND A LIFETIME

Gretchen's experience beautifully illustrates the way spiritual healing can open the door for powerful whole-person recovery from self-inflicted violence. You may not have articulated it like this, but you probably picked up this book because you want the self-harmer in your life to experience the same kind of total healing Gretchen did.

I don't know what the self-injurer you love believes about God. For that matter, I don't know where you stand on issues of spirituality. I expressed in the introduction and have indicated throughout this book that the redemptive narrative of Jesus Christ is radically transforming, and without it, true wholeness does not exist. I fully believe that beginning and nurturing an authentic and truth-based relationship with God is key for the self-wounder you care about.

But as Gretchen's story shows, discovering and embracing faith in God does not solve everything. The urge to self-injure did not immediately cease for Gretchen. Acknowledging God did not liberate her from the ache of shame, anger, and hopeless desperation.

It would be wonderful if once a person came into a hope-filling relationship with God, all his or her broken means of self-protection and self-help would magically disappear. From experience or observation, however, most of us know this does not happen.

Pastor Chuck Swindoll articulates this well: "Conversion is a miracle of a moment; sanctification [which we might loosely define as being changed from the inside out] is a process of a lifetime."[2]

In conversion, a person recognizes and places faith in God as the Way, the Truth, and the Life. As many of us have accepted, the biblical story of redemption is, on the most fundamental level, one of a suffering Love who ultimately triumphs over pain. It is a tale in which peace does prevail and love does conquer all. But also woven throughout this victorious narrative are the bloody and heart-wrenching wounds of sin, those others commit and those we ourselves choose.

Through the process of sanctification, people grow into their belief in a God who brings beauty from these wounds and hope for the hopeless.

182

Spiritual healing for the self-injurer you love comes through embarking on and persevering in this journey of growth. People like you can play a crucial role in a self-harmer's quest for spiritual healing by encouraging and modeling for this person a commitment to sanctification.

As we've seen throughout this book, learning to deal with pain is absolutely essential for self-wounders. In order for people who use self-inflicted violence as a coping mechanism to mature spiritually and experience the victory of a loving God, they must come up with a healthy response to suffering.

In journeying toward God and with God, self-injurers may—somewhat ironically—have an advantage over people who have grown up in relatively happy surroundings insulated from suffering. Self-harmers like Gretchen know that the world is broken. Many of them sense—in the most acute ways—that *they* are broken. Self-injurers often more readily acknowledge the truth that humanity and pain are inextricably linked in every soul.

But sensing this broken neediness in the world and in their own hearts, self-injurers feel compelled to come up with an answer for suffering. Unfortunately, one of the most common responses to woundedness—a sense of deep and persistent shame—often feeds into the vicious cycle of self-inflicted violence. It forms a complex barrier to spiritual healing. So to understand and help the self-harmers in our lives, let's consider the role of shame in their suffering.

A HUNK OF LEAD ON THE HEART

Theologian Lewis Smedes offers one of the best and most heartbreakingly vivid definitions of shame I have come across. He writes, "Shame is a vague, undefined heaviness that presses on our spirit, dampens our gratitude for the goodness of life, and slackens the free flow of joy. Shame is a primal feeling, the kind that seeps into and discolors all our other feelings, primarily about ourself but about almost everyone and everything else in our life as well."[3]

Shame is a nebulous and primal sense that stains everything around us and infects almost every one of us. Shame proves an especially strong force in the lives of self-wounders. Think back with me over the stories self-injurers have shared with us in this book.

Do you remember the deadening weight of shame Joy felt because of her cutting, bulimia, and masturbation? Beth felt as though she would never escape the shame of sexual abuse at the hands of her grandfather. And Ed, the dangerously obsessive exerciser, experienced heartrending shame after his mother's affair and abandonment.

Smedes further illuminates shame with these words: "Shame . . . is a feeling that we do not measure up and maybe never will measure up to the sorts of persons we are meant to be. The feeling, when we are conscious of it, gives us a vague disgust with ourselves, which in turn feels like a hunk of lead on our hearts."[4]

For self-injurers, vague disgust often escalates into a pervasive shame that speaks wickedly painful messages to the heart: "You're defective, worthless, inadequate. There's nothing good in you." Shame attacks the core of our very selves: It focuses not on a bad thing we've done or said but on who we are.

John Bradshaw articulates well this "most destructive aspect of shame . . . the process whereby shame moves from being a feeling to being a state of being." He observes, "Once we internalize a shame message, we make conclusions about ourselves based on that message. The effect can be devastating."[5]

Shame annihilates the self. It rips the last thread of dignity from the heart in a violent assault. It prevents us from asking for and receiving forgiveness because we fear it will make us feel worse to admit our faults or recognize the lies we've believed. Shame ultimately causes people, especially self-harmers, to despise themselves vehemently and hold themselves in unrelenting contempt.

Self-contempt gives people something to focus their pain and shame on: themselves. If people believe they are unworthy of love or happiness, they won't be disappointed. If people believe they deserve to be abused, they have an explanation for the pain they experience at the hands of others.

Shame roots itself in the heart through a wide variety of channels. Some of the most common are shaming messages from graceless religion, unaccepting parents or other influential people, and a culture that constantly reminds us that we are not good enough and may never be. The Enemy of our souls also piles shame on our hearts. You may have heard that his name, Satan, literally means "accuser." Satan blames people for causing their own misery and convinces them that they deserve the agony in their lives.

Childhood abuse heaps shame on its victims. People feel ashamed of their weaknesses, whether they are perfectionists trying to hide their flaws or they suffer from a depression they cannot explain. Shame infects people rejected and abandoned by loved ones. It robs people of their God-given dignity and inherent, unique worth.

Psychologists Dr. Dan Allender and Dr. Tremper Longman III remind us that humans were not created for self-condemnation. In their masterful book *The Cry of the Soul*, Allender and Longman note,

> Contempt is an assault against the glory God intends His children to bear. It sears and stings. . . . Contempt is a poison that paralyzes our deepest longing for love and meaning, stripping us of hope. It mocks our desirability: "No one wants you. No one enjoys you." . . . Contempt isolates its victims by branding them unworthy of love. . . . After dividing and isolating, contempt withers hope by making its victim feel foolish, deadening desire.[6]

Shame's wicked and illogical nature divides the world into "good" and "bad" people. Shame doesn't use reason. It just makes us *feel* bad. But ultimately, there are no "good" or "bad" people. There are only broken people.

Many of us have heard since childhood that every human was

created to reflect the radiant image of God. Yet we all know or sub-consciously sense that His image in us has been and continues to be shattered by the hurtful things we and others think, do, and say. Many of us are people bound by shame who cannot live out the beauty and love for which we were designed.

When it comes to self-injury, shame plays an interesting role for both the self-harmer and the people in his or her life who feel, even if unwillingly, ashamed of the behavior and sense they may have contrib-uted to the self-wounder's shame.

You may have responded to the suffering caused by another's choice of self-inflicted violence by shaming him or her. Every one of us com-municates—at one time or another—shaming messages to those we love. Freedom begins in recognizing, "No matter how hard I try, I won't always be what my family needs. I've made mistakes and will continue making them. I have either unintentionally or willfully shamed the people I love, and I will face responsibility for the problems of the past, the issues of today, and those that will arise in the future."

Humans do not innately know how to deal with shame. But we can learn to combat the toxic beliefs that cause us to doubt and wound ourselves. Whenever shame attacks us, no matter what the reason, we come to a crossroad. A choices lies before us: Will we rush to find relief for ourselves, or will we rely on something greater than ourselves?

THE WEIGHTLESSNESS OF GRACE

If shame loads a hunk of dead weight on our souls, how can we ourselves experience and help self-injurers in our lives live in freedom from the heaviness of shame? The answer comes in recognizing and embracing the life force that opposes and triumphs over shame: grace.

Psychoanalyst Gerhart Piers pioneered the current understand-ing of shame through years of research. In his work *Shame and Guilt*, Piers informs us that beneath the feelings of shame, one inevitably finds fear of abandonment. Carl Schneider, author of *Shame, Exposure, and*

Privacy, concurs: "The underlying dynamic of . . . shame is the fear of rejection."[7]

In the end, acceptance is the single most compelling need of our lives. The self-wounders you love desperately long, as all humans do, to be affirmed, valued, and cherished. Shame tells them that they cannot be accepted because they are not acceptable; they are too bad, beyond fixing.

But Lewis Smedes says, "Grace overcomes shame . . . simply by accepting us, the whole of us, with no regard to our beauty or our ugliness, our virtue or our vices. We are accepted wholesale. Accepted with no possibility of being rejected. Accepted once and accepted forever. Accepted at the ultimate depth of our being. We are given what we have longed for in every nook and nuance of every relationship."[8]

Helping self-harmers accept grace answers and overcomes shame. It provides the thing Smedes says we need most: "to be accepted without regard to whether we are acceptable." Smedes continues, "We experience grace as power: it provides a spiritual energy to shed the heaviness of shame and, in the lightness of grace, move toward [and enjoy] the true self God means us to be."[9]

Grace empowers us to courageously look at the complex messiness of shadow and light in the world around us and in ourselves. It then allows us to embrace the good news that we can be accepted, fully and irreversibly, no matter what our past or present, no matter what unacceptable things we might do in the future. Nothing we can do can keep God, the very definition of grace, from accepting us because He forgives us for all the things we do and accepts us for all that we are.

Grace heals our shame by removing what shame causes us to fear most: rejection and abandonment. Grace gives us a sense of worth and value that no shadow within us (and we *all* know those shadows within us) can revoke.

This is the weightless beauty of grace. And it is the message we can communicate to the self-injurers we love. We can invite shame-burdened people, as Jesus does, to exchange the heaviness of shame for

His gracious lightness. He invites us: "Are you tired? Worn out? . . . Come to me. Get away with me and you'll recover your life. I'll show you how to take a real rest. Walk with me and work with me—watch how I do it. Learn the unforced rhythms of grace. I won't lay anything heavy or ill-fitting on you. Keep company with me and you'll learn to live freely and lightly" (Matthew 11:28-30, MSG).

Insidiously, shame tells self-injurers that they are unworthy of grace, of the freedom and lightness they crave. One way we can help self-harmers live in grace is by communicating to them what God says about who they are. The Bible speaks clearly to the dignity of *every* human. As your loved ones battle self-injury through psychological and physiological treatment, you can concurrently help them live in the reality of who they are as God's children:

- *Chosen, holy, and dearly loved.* Colossians 3:12 reveals, "God chose you to be the holy people he loves." When the self-injurers you love feel that no one wants them and everyone thinks they're worthless or unlovable, you can help them cling to this truth.
- *Treasures of infinite value.* First Corinthians 6:20 teaches us that "God bought you with a high price." We can help self-harmers accept and experience the truth that Christ's life, death, and resurrection prove they are worth more to God than they can even comprehend.
- *"Wonderfully complex."* These are the words the New Living Translation uses in Psalm 139:14 to render the description God gives of His human creations. We can continually remind our loved ones that God made them "in an amazing and wonderful way" (Psalm 139:14, NCV). Who they are brings delight to their Creator. He loves that they have so many thoughts, feelings, and passions. He does not want them to shut off their emotions in an icy numbness that may block pain but also locks away joy and peace and love.

- *Equipped to face fear and pain.* Second Timothy 1:7 proclaims this glorious truth: "God has not given us a spirit of fear and timidity, but of power, love, and self-discipline." We can help self-harmers recognize that they don't have to shrink in the face of fear or of any self-injurious impulse. They have been given a spirit of strength, love, and self-control, and they have the spiritual power to exercise those "muscles."

Working in concert, these truths (and others) help self-wounders live the life they were created to live—a life free of self-condemnation and self-harm. As we remember these transforming words and as we speak them into the lives of self-harmers, we can help them reject the messages and feelings of shame that have burdened them so heavily. We can help them do this by encouraging them to incorporate God's words into their vocabulary and into the fabric of their minds. His language does not speak shame, but hope.

Through the prophet Isaiah, God proclaims to both self-injurers and those close to them, "Don't be afraid—you're not going to be embarrassed. Don't hold back—you're not going to come up short. You'll forget all about the humiliations of your youth" (Isaiah 54:4, MSG). But we cannot stop short of helping self-injurers reject the messages of shame, because through life-giving knowledge, God ultimately allows us to *experience*, not simply "know about," truth. As many of us know, authentic freedom comes when the knowledge in our head moves to our heart. To encourage this, you can help self-wounders learn to do the following.

Feel what they know about God.

Self-harmers, particularly those who have grown up in the church, may know a lot about God. They may be able to recite verses about God's love for them and Jesus' suffering love. But the connection between their head and heart has often been lost.

God doesn't want self-injurers to simply know His promises (or poke holes in them: *Yeah, yeah, yeah, God loves me, but . . .*). He longs to engage with their hearts; He longs for them to *feel* His love and grace. God could have chosen to create humans without the capacity to feel at all, but in fashioning us in His image, the God who loves and grieves and gets righteously angry gave us the wonderfully bitter-sweet gift of feelings. The self-harmers you care about have experienced dark and frightening emotions. It may seem easier for them to hide or ignore or cut away the feelings that keep them captive to fear, rage, self-contempt, and doubt in God. But the Spirit longs to unlock the corners of their minds and hearts that house forbidding emotions. We can encourage self-wounders to take the risk and allow their darkest feelings to be exposed to God, who trades heaviness for weightlessness and clarifies the genuine dignity of their lives.

Most of us, at some time or another, have felt afraid to express—even to God—what we truly feel, think, and desire. But Dan Allender so beautifully reminds us that "prayer does not inform God; rather, it draws us into His presence and invites Him into our life."[10]

Live out the truth.

I think Dallas Willard speaks to this issue brilliantly: "To believe something is to act as if it is so. To believe that two plus two equals four is to behave accordingly when trying to find out how many apples or dollars are in the house. The advantage of believing it is not that we can pass tests in arithmetic; it is that we can deal much more successfully with reality."[11]

We can help self-harmers see that they do not *learn* truth so that they can answer questions in Sunday school or respond correctly when someone asks them, "What does God say about that?"

Instead, they *live in* truth so they can deal much more successfully with reality, with the problem of pain.

Truth reveals Himself in an infinite number of ways. I wish I could outline all the bondage-breaking promises of God that apply to self-injurious tendencies. But since I cannot, let me outline a few key truths that you can help self-harmers embrace:[12]

- *By His wounds they are healed.* We can proclaim to self-injurers the truth that Ephesians 2:13 declares: "Though you once were far away from God, now you have been brought near to him because of the blood of Christ." And we can help them embrace the beauty of Isaiah 53:5: "The punishment, which made us well, was given to him, and we are healed because of his wounds" (NCV).

- *Christ has completed everything necessary to assure their protection and salvation.* In John 19:30, Christ cried out from the cross, "'It is finished.' Then he bowed his head and gave up his spirit" (NRSV). His body was broken, battered, and wounded so that self-harmers' bodies do not have to be. He has done everything needed—everything that will *ever be* needed—to make right the wrong things they've done and the wrong things others have done to them. I love this freeing truth, words of hope that we can share with self-injurers we love: "'Their sins and lawless acts I will remember no more.' And where these have been forgiven, there is no longer any sacrifice for sin" (Hebrews 10:17-18, NIV).

- *God truly understands them.* As Hebrews 4:15 tells us, "We don't have a priest who is out of touch with our reality. He's been through weakness and testing, experienced it all—all but the sin" (MSG). On the cross, Christ suffered physically. He understands bodily pain. But He also experienced incomprehensible emotional grief. He knows what it feels like to be completely abandoned by His family (see Mark 15:34), to be abused and mistreated (see Isaiah 53:3-5), and to feel so crushed by grief that death seems imminent. He understands overwhelming sorrow (see Matthew 26:38). He knows their desire to escape suffering. He has been through it all, and we can help self-harmers remember and cling to these truths.

- *God is available to them.* We can share this wonderful truth with self-wounders we love: Unbelievably, because of Christ's sacrifice, they have access to the Almighty. Hebrews 4:16 encourages us all: "Walk right up to him and get what he is so ready to give. Take the mercy, accept the help" (MSG). We can help self-injurers see that they don't have a God who sits silently by as they suffer. God is ready to give help, ready to cover them with mercy. We can continually remind them that God is available to them.

- *God uses their pain to proclaim His strength.* Second Corinthians 12:9 allows the self-harmers we care about to set aside perfectionistic or despair-driven performance forever. God promises, "My grace is enough for you. When you are weak, my power is made perfect in you" (NCV). In verse 10 of the same chapter, Paul rejoices that "when I am weak, then I am truly strong" (NCV). We can help self-wounders live in the truths that they do not have to be the "strong one"; they do not have to hold everything together. In fact, when they allow themselves to be weak, they can experience His power more fully.

- *God is honored even by their questions.* I like how Dan Allender and Tremper Longman so aptly note, "The irony of questioning God is that it honors Him: it turns our hearts away from ungodly despair toward a passionate desire to comprehend Him."[13] Even in self-harmers' doubts about His goodness, even in the hollowness of their loss and pain, if they continue to engage with God, He *will* faithfully reveal Himself. Sometimes we need to help others see (and need to be reminded ourselves) that God blesses those who persistently pursue Him, even in the face of silent disappointment. Read Luke 11:5-13 and 18:1-8 for great examples of this.

- *God has started and promises to complete His redeeming work in them.* Paul reassures us that "God began doing a good work in you, and I am sure he will continue it until it is finished when Jesus Christ comes again" (Philippians 1:6, NCV). When your loved ones fear they will never overcome the desire to self-injure, when you feel nothing will get better, this truth can restore hope.

Though it's a process that requires revisiting them over and over again, really living in these truths will diminish the urge in those we love to choose self-inflicted violence. Self-harm will lose some of its appeal when the lightness of gracious acceptance transforms those we love.

And there are some other practical spiritual steps we can help self-injurers pursue, steps that will help them experience the grace that heals and restores.

Pray and meditate.

It has been said that through prayer we communicate with God, and in meditation we allow Him to communicate with us. Prayer and meditation help restore the inner peace that He longs for us to experience. We can help self-harmers learn these spiritual disciplines. And as an amazing physiological bonus, prayer and meditation actually promote endorphin release, decrease physical pain, and help reduce muscle tension. Both the person who feels drawn to self-inflicted violence and you who live in the tension of loving a self-injurer will benefit from using these essential outlets. For an excellent discussion of and instruction in prayer and meditation, you can refer to Richard Foster's classic books *Prayer* and *Celebration of Discipline*.

Receive the ministry of presence.

Mark 5:1-20 records the tragic existence of one self-injurer. Most people avoided the man who lived in the tombs and repeatedly slashed himself with rocks. But Jesus came to him and showered him with compassion. Through His life, Christ taught that being with people who are hurting *matters*. We all know that it's easier to ignore the hurt in other people than it is to get into the pit with them. But Christ models how to and challenges us to give and receive the ministry of presence. Simply being with self-harmers makes a big difference, but self-injurers often feel unworthy of this ministry. We can help self-wounders tremendously by giving the gift of presence whenever possible.

Practice and enjoy the ministry of incarnation.

Do you remember Natalie, who shared with us her poetry and her seven-year battle with self-harm? Her road to recovery included significant time exploring faith and spiritual transformation. And Natalie found that in taking Communion, she experienced the healing power of Christ's incarnation.

She explained to me,

> Sometimes the only thing that got me through the week was the Eucharist[14] on Sunday and the symbolism of deep truths there. Taking Christ's body into mine and acknowledging that my body is holy now and belongs to God, that I am in fact a part of the body of Christ, meant so much. It made me realize that when I harm my body I am harming the body of Christ. The wine [symbolizing] Christ's blood coming inside me and cleansing every part of me reminded me it was done. I am clean, I am forgiven, and there is nothing else I have to prove. In the end I think it is the value that God's love and sacrifice confer on me that has helped me change my view of myself and my body.

We can share Communion with self-harmers we love and encourage them to remember Christ's victory over pain in the Eucharist. They may experience the same deep healing Natalie did.

Confront the darkness.

This is an extraordinarily difficult idea to discuss without offending or angering some people. There are those who believe that self-injury is primarily, or only, an issue of spiritual warfare. They use words like *demonic influence*, *oppression*, and *possession* to talk about self-inflicted violence and the people who struggle with it. Others scoff at these terms and the very idea that "evil forces" can influence people to do or think anything.

I firmly believe in the existence of evil and in an Enemy of the human soul. But whether or not you believe in evil or the work of evil in the universe, it's critical in a book on self-harm that we address the deep sense of darkness that many self-wounders feel. Some speak of this palpable darkness as a "presence" or "force" within and around them.

Though his memoir, *A Million Little Pieces*, was exposed as a better piece of fiction than history, James Frey writes about this phenomenon powerfully. He calls it "the Fury" and explains, "It flows through my veins like a slow, lazy virus, urging me to do damage. . . . I want it to go away. I want it to leave me. When [the Fury] is at its full, I am often at its mercy, but not now. I know what to do to make it go away; I know how to make it disappear. Feed it pain and it will leave me. Feed it pain and it will go away."[15]

Lorel, a self-wounder who shared her story in *Ophelia Speaks*, describes a similar sense:

> My life is a tunnel. A spiral of darkness, depression, and death. My descent down is eternal. I almost feel claws around my wrists and ankles pulling me down deeper. They are burning my flesh. The light at the top is fading along with the image of Jesus above. I try to stretch my fingertips upwards begging, pleading for him to see me and rescue me. Evidently I am not screaming loud enough, because he never does answer my prayers.[16]

If you're anything like me, these words both break your heart and terrify you at the same time. It's unnerving, even frightening to think that people we love may feel a similar sense of darkness around and inside them.

In order to help self-harmers confront the darkness they live in, we can courageously listen as they tell their stories. We can help reiterate, over and over again, words of truth, hope, mercy, and love into their lives, all of which combat and oppose the darkness. And we can encourage them to actively battle anything that attacks their mind and body.

If you feel that you're in over your head regarding this spiritual darkness, seek the counsel of a trusted mentor or pastor. Getting some objective advice from a person who may know more than you do about the palpable darkness some self-injurers face is a brave and important thing to do.

I recognize that this section may leave some of you feeling frustrated. But this book is not about identifying instances of spiritual warfare or demonic influence. I cannot differentiate between or define the role (or lack thereof) of possession and oppression in your friend/family member/loved one's self-inflicted violence. I can, however, encourage you to listen attentively and act on the information that self-wounders offer about the darkness they feel and fear.

Use the tools they've been given.

Praise God that neither we nor the self-injurers we love have to wage war on our own strength. In 2 Corinthians 10:4, Paul reveals, "Our weapons have power from God that can destroy the enemy's strong places" (NCV).

Verses 5 and 6 then exhort us to "use our powerful God-tools for smashing warped philosophies, tearing down barriers erected against the truth of God, fitting every loose thought and emotion and impulse into the structure of life shaped by Christ. Our tools are ready at hand for clearing the ground of every obstruction and building lives of obedience into maturity" (MSG).

None of us has to fight this fearsome battle against self-inflicted violence by ourselves. We have been given the weapons of the Almighty Lord of hosts, the Commander of the heavenly armies.

We can help self-wounders grab hold of their inheritance — the tools God's given His children to fit *every* self-injurious thought and emotion and impulse into a life shaped by Christ. Ephesians 6:10-18 gives us an incredible description of the weapons that are ours; this passage may be a powerful one to share with the self-injurer in your life.

Confess and repent.

Among self-harmers, confession and repentance suffer pretty poor reputations. Images of shame, anger, and punishment often come to mind. But while they think admitting their faults will lead them to condemnation and despair, it actually allows them to fully experience the radical, undeserved love that heals.

Our God is ever ready to forgive. Psalm 130:3-4 reassures us:

> If you . . . kept a record of sins,
> O Lord, who could stand?
> But with you there *is* forgiveness. (NIV, emphasis added)

I would also love to share with every self-wounder this paraphrase of the gracious promise found in Psalm 103:10: "He is grieved when we . . . fail, but He quickly draws us to His forgiving heart and accepts us just as if it never happened."[17]

Eugene Peterson describes our lives as arrows that point either toward or away from God. And when any of us (whether we misuse work or shopping or choose self-inflicted violence to numb pain) mistakenly acts on the belief that self-protective, self-preserving, or self-punishing behaviors will help us live, the arrows of our lives shift in the wrong direction. We no longer point toward the Source of life, but rather toward the source of the very suffering we're trying to avoid.

Repenting of any wrong, including self-injurious behaviors, requires humility and committed movement toward the real Source. But it also includes wild celebration in the truth that grace lifts us from our brokenness. Awareness of our own neediness is one of God's most paradoxical gifts.

In one of the most powerful, life-changing narratives in the Bible, what we often call the parable of the Prodigal Son (see Luke 15:11-32), Jesus describes the kind of true repentance we can help self-harmers learn and practice. I love the way Dan Allender exposits this parable in his book *The Wounded Heart*. He explains that repentance often begins with the recognition that the things people thought would preserve their lives (things like self-inflicted violence) have, in fact, landed them in the pigpen. Allender writes, "Repentance . . . clears the senses in a way that exposes depravity and affirms dignity. It awakens our hunger for our Father's embrace and deepens our awareness of His kind involvement. And when we are deeply, truly touched by His love, we will move boldly" into the "sweet joy of restoration."[18]

Self-injury, like *every* attempt to live apart from God, springs from broken, sinful humanity. The Lord did not create us to harm ourselves but to delight in our bodies and care for them. As Paul exhorts in 1 Corinthians 6:13, "Since the Master honors you with a body, honor him with your body!" (MSG).

Self-harmers often believe they are preserving their life by cutting, burning, or breaking pain from their body. We can help those who engage in self-inflicted violence live in the truth that their injurious behavior never gives life. It robs them of the joy of living with the Father. All of our own attempts to live apart from the Father destroy us as well.

As we have noted often throughout this chapter, self-wounders fear that God will not receive them because they are "too bad." They may even try to clean up their behavior before returning to the Father. We have the privilege of reminding the self-injurers we love that God does not condition their value on their behavior — *ever*. Like the father in the parable of the Prodigal Son, He waits for them to return, runs to them, throws His arms around them, and invites them to celebrate real life with Him.

We can help them see repentance as "melting into the warm arms of God, acknowledging the wonder of being received when it would be so understandable to be spurned, . . . taking [their] place at the great feast, . . . and delighting in the undeserved party being held in honor of [their] return."[19] Repentance is met with full restoration and celebration.

This is an incredibly difficult truth to live out. It's been ingrained in so many self-harmers that God's primary desire is that they toe the line, acting like "good little boys and girls."

We can model for self-wounders the truth that God longs for more than our good behavior. He wants all of us to live in the truth that He is the Source, the *only* Source, of life. We all resort to broken, sinful methods at some point in our lives. If you will risk modeling true repentance, self-injurers will see how they, too, can acknowledge their desperate attempts to live apart from God and His desire that we return to celebrate grace with Him.

Practice the art of forgiveness.

Philosopher Hannah Arendt once wrote, "The only possible redemption from the predicament of being unable to undo what one has done . . . is the faculty of forgiving."[20]

Many, many of the self-injurers in our lives have been continually shamed, brutally abused, and/or cruelly rejected by others. A long-fermenting bitterness against the people who infected them with shame, fear, and pain can rob them of joy for a lifetime.

None of us can undo what others have done to us. And we cannot alter the reality that we have been wronged and now carry the memories of past wounds around with us. Self-wounders often fight against an unbearable tide of resentment.

For self-injurers, like for all of us, the only path out of bitterness is the difficult road of forgiveness. If you know self-harmers who battle bitterness, the last thing they may want to hear is that forgiveness will set them free.

They may fear it will trivialize or dismiss what they went through. Forgiving may seem weak to them. Perhaps they don't believe that the person who hurt them deserves to be forgiven. And on that last count, they would be perfectly accurate. While forgiveness is not weak and does not absolve the other person of responsibility, it *is* true that people do not "deserve" forgiveness.

No one deserves to be forgiven. Even saying we're sorry does not earn us the right to be forgiven. Forgiveness springs only out of a Love that theologians call grace—unmerited, unwarranted mercy.

We, too, stand in need of forgiveness. We are not above the people who hurt us. We are not merely innocent bystanders. In life we wound and are wounded. When we can see ourselves as flawed, like others, we may be better able to forgive as God forgives us.

With radical mercy, Jesus introduced an ethic higher than "an eye for an eye." As He cried from the cross, "Father, forgive them, for they do not know what they are doing" (Luke 23:34, NIV), Christ showed us how to forgive—mercifully, completely, and *unconditionally*.

This does not mean the self-injurers we love have to tolerate what happened to them. They do not have to deny the depth of their wounds or absolve those who injured them from the demands of justice.

No; we can remind them that true and godly forgiveness is brutally honest. It recognizes the depth of the hurt and acknowledges the wrongness of it. But we can also help them see that forgiveness does not take matters into its own hands.

What they can do, instead, is let *God* settle the score. They can allow the Judge to enforce His laws. And we can encourage self-harmers to remember that they can trust, even when they do not see God's justice come to those who injured them, that He *always* acts justly.[21]

No doubt about it, forgiveness is difficult. Smedes likens it to spiritual surgery on our own souls. He also rightly claims that sometimes the thing changed by our willingness to forgive is our own feelings. This is often a bitter pill to swallow: We cannot control how the people who offend us will respond to our mercy.

Blessedly, we can help self-injurers see that the surgery of forgiveness heals. We can help them live in the truth that no matter what happened to them in the past, their memories can be lost in the sea of God's mercy. Through forgiveness, they can be set free.

JOY IN THE JOURNEY

I realize this is a lot to digest. And that's why it's refreshing to remember that sanctification is a process that spans a lifetime. Healing doesn't have to happen all at once. The self-injurer you love will be transformed from the inside for the rest of his or her life.

Our joy in the journey is this: The rewards of spiritual growth are worth it. Jesus came so that we and the self-harmers we love "can have real and eternal life, more and better life than [we] ever dreamed of" (John 10:10, MSG).

By His wounds, and His wounds alone, we experience and can share with others the abundantly rich life He died to give. In Christ Jesus, all wisdom—medical, psychological, and scriptural—comes into fullness of life.

He yearns for all of us to recognize the broken neediness of our bodies, minds, and spirits. He aches that we might know His strength and find it to be sufficient. This is where healing, for the self-injurer and for *every* human, begins.

A BENEDICTION

That one whose faith is focused on God,
who finds his security in Him,
does not have to live in fear.

He is not left untouched
by the tempest of life,
and he may be wounded
by the onslaughts of evil,

But his great God does not leave him
to suffer these things alone.

The Lord cares for His own and delivers him
even in the midst of the conflicts
that plague him.

If God is truly your God,
you do not have to be afraid
of . . . the affliction that lays you low. . . .

The Lord is by your side
to raise you to your feet

and to lead you to ultimate victory. . . .

Our loving God has promised it:

"Because My child loves Me,
I will not let him go.

I shall feel the pain of his wounds
and bear his hurt
and shall transform that which is ugly
into that which enriches and blesses.

And when he cries out in agony,
I shall hear him.

I will be close to him and will deliver him
and I will grant him eternal life." (Psalm 91)[1]

APPENDIX A

Finding a Therapist

Things to look for:

- A person who integrates mental, physical, and spiritual healing
- A therapist who feels comfortable working with self-injurers (sadly, many counselors are not willing to take on self-wounding clients)
- A clinician who balances a supportive and nurturing approach to therapy with a firm and directive one (this will help break down cycles of denial and/or manipulation common to self-harmers)
- An individual trained in dealing with crisis emotions and situations
- A therapist who fits within your budget (many professionals work with insurance companies or on a sliding scale for clients in need)
- A counselor recommended by others (you will almost always have better luck finding a good counselor through a referral than through the yellow pages)

If you aren't sure how to locate this kind of professional, you can call Focus on the Family at (800) 232-6459 ext. 7700 (8 a.m. to 5 p.m.

INSIDE A CUTTER'S MIND

MST) for a free referral to a counselor in your area. Your local place of worship or community center may provide referrals as well.

Suggested questions to ask before you decide on a therapist:

- What is your basic philosophy of therapy?
- Do you specialize in any particular area?
- What kind of experience have you had treating people with self-inflicted violence? What is your basic philosophy regarding self-injury?
- Do you incorporate group and/or family therapy in a recovery plan? How do you do this?
- How do you feel about working alongside a medical doctor (general practitioner, psychiatrist, neurologist, etc.) I or my loved one will see concurrently?
- What is your view on using medication to treat self-injury?
- How do you feel about other forms of treatment I or my loved one is interested in (for example, biofeedback, EMDR, DBT, SPECT scanning)?
- Do you require payment at time of service, or are you willing to wait for insurance reimbursement?
- Is there anything else you think I should know about you or the way you do therapy?

APPENDIX B
ADDITIONAL RESOURCES AND CONTACT INFORMATION

Outstanding websites specifically devoted to understanding and recovering from self-injury:

- http://www.selfharm.net (Secret Shame: Self-Injury Information and Support)
- www.siari.co.uk (SIARI: Self-Injury & Related Issues for the international community)
- www.selfinjury.org (The American Self-Harm Information Clearinghouse)
- www.self-injury.org (the Lysamena Project on Self-Injury: Christian-based self-injury information and resources)

For more information about treatment options:

SPECT BRAIN IMAGING

Amen Clinics, Inc.
4019 Westerly Place, Suite 100
Newport Beach, CA 92660
Telephone: 1-949-266-3700
E-mail: contact@amenclinic.com
Online: www.amenclinics.com

MUTUAL-HELP GROUPS

Self Mutilators Anonymous (SMA)
E-mail: info@selfmutilatorsanonymous.org
Online: http://www.selfmutilatorsanonymous.org/
Note: Along with meetings in specific areas, SMA hosts online meetings and conference-call meetings.

Overcomers Outreach
P.O. Box 922950
Sylmar, CA 91392-2950
Telephone: 1-800-310-3001 or 1-877-9OVERCOME
E-mail: info@overcomersoutreach.org
Online: www.overcomersoutreach.org

Celebrate Recovery (originally started at Saddleback Church in Southern California, now worldwide)
Celebrate Recovery Books
25422 Trabuco Road #105-151
Lake Forest, CA 92630
Telephone: 1-949-581-0548
Online: http://www.celebraterecovery.com/

GOVERNMENT-SPONSORED MENTAL-HEALTH RESOURCES

National Coalition of Mental Health Professionals and Consumers, Inc.
P.O. Box 438
Commack, New York 11725

Telephone: 1-866-8-COALITION (1-866-826-2548) or 1-631-979-5307
Fax: 1-631-979-5293
E-mail: Kathleen Saccardi, office manager, at NCMHPC@aol.com
Online: http://www.thenationalcoalition.org/

EYE MOVEMENT DESENSITIZATION AND REPROCESSING (EMDR)

EMDR International Association
5806 Mesa Drive, Suite 360
Austin, Texas 78731
Telephone: 1-866-451-5200 or 1-512-451-5200
Fax: 1-512-451-5256
E-mail: info@emdria.org
Online: www.emdria.org

DIALECTICAL BEHAVIOR THERAPY (DBT)

Behavioral Tech
4556 University Way NE, Suite 200
Seattle, WA 98105
Telephone: 1-206-675-8588
E-mail: information@behavioraltech.org
Online: http://www.behavioraltech.com/crd

PSYCHOLOGICAL TESTING

American Psychological Association
750 First Street, NE
Washington, DC 20002-4242
Telephone: 1-800-374-2721 or 1-202-336-5500
Online: http://www.apa.org/science/faq-findtests
.html

BIOFEEDBACK

The Association for Applied Psychophysiology and
Biofeedback (formerly the Biofeedback Research
Society)
10200 West 44th Avenue, Suite 304
Wheat Ridge, CO 80033
Phone: 1-800-477-8892 or 1-303-422-8436
Fax: 1-303-422-8894
E-mail: aapb@resourcenter.com
Online: http://www.aapb.org

APPENDIX C

Alternatives to Self-Injurious Behavior[1]

Note: Different emotions need different expressions. When the person you love feels anxious or angry, watching a movie may not be the best idea. Instead, you might want to suggest going to the gym or tearing up old phone books. On the other hand, when someone feels weary or depressed, swimming might not sound exciting. Quietly coloring or reading aloud might be better options. If you'd like, you can mark next to each of the following suggestions the emotions you think would best be relieved by the activity.

This list provides suggestions of activities self-harmers can do either on their own or together with you, particularly when self-injurious urges are heightened. The list is rather extensive. In crisis times, it's difficult to plow through a list this long. So it may be a good idea to highlight in advance the things that seem particularly interesting to you and your loved one. Then you can create a "short list" of activities to do.

- Listening to favorite music
- Making music (singing out loud or playing an instrument actually releases endorphins!)
- Creating something
    - ☐ Drawing or painting
    - ☐ Sculpting (do you remember how fun

Play-Doh and Silly Putty can be?)
☐ Painting ceramics or designing pottery
☐ Making a home movie
☐ Woodworking
☐ Crocheting or knitting
☐ Doing needlework
☐ Coloring (buy some coloring books and crayons)

- Writing

☐ A letter or e-mail to someone you love (including yourself and God)
☐ In a journal
☐ Creatively (a poem, play, or short story, perhaps)
☐ A memoir or autobiography of your life thus far
☐ A biography of an influential and inspiring person in your life

- Exercising

☐ Cycling
☐ Going to the batting cages
☐ Hitting golf balls (best to do this at a range)
☐ Swimming
☐ Climbing
☐ Skating
☐ Skateboarding
☐ Yoga
☐ Pilates
☐ Sailing
☐ Hiking
☐ Walking
☐ Jogging
☐ Aerobics

□ Punching a punching bag
□ Lifting weights
□ Stretching
□ Bowling
□ Frisbee
□ Participating in a team sport (there are almost always pickup games at local courts)

- Gardening (pulling weeds may be an especially good tension reliever)
- Cleaning or fixing something (this works especially well if you are a detail-oriented person and if the task is an engrossing one)
- Cooking
- Taking a drive
- Taking a ride on the subway, bus, or train
- Helping someone else

    □ Volunteering in your community
    □ Offering to serve a friend or neighbor in need

- Petting, grooming, or playing with an animal (stuffed animals can work too)
- Spending time in the sun

    □ Playing with squirt guns
    □ Throwing water balloons

- Cuddling with someone you love
- Exercising your brain

    □ Puzzles
    □ Crosswords
    □ Word finds
    □ Hidden pictures

- Shopping (and remember, window-shopping or bargain hunting can be just as fun and is certainly easier on your finances)
- Making a list (and then researching online or elsewhere)

    □ Places you would like to visit

        ☐ Things you would like to do
- Playing with hair
  - ☐ Styling it
  - ☐ Dying it
- Going to an art gallery or museum
- Looking at your own or other people's photo albums
- Watching old home movies
- Eating or drinking something enjoyable (but it's important to avoid caffeine when you are emotionally escalated)
- Repeating verses or prayers to yourself
  - ☐ Example: "God is our refuge and strength, always ready to help in times of trouble." (Psalm 46:1)
  - ☐ Passages from the Book of Common Prayer or another source
- Using markers (washable markers are best) to draw on your skin
- Taking a shower or bath (get rid of razors before you get in)
- Counting backward slowly
- Practicing deep breathing (a good technique is to place a tissue box on your stomach and watch the rise and fall of your breath until you feel more relaxed)
- Naming five things you like to see, smell, touch, taste, and hear
- Touching something familiar and safe (a blanket, animal, or token that reminds you of a happy time)
- Meditating (listening to God)
- Praying (talking to God)
- Going to the library
- Visiting a historic site near you
- Reading something life-affirming (you may offer to read aloud to someone who's tired)
  - ☐ The Bible stories you loved during childhood
  - ☐ A redemptive novel

  ☐ An inspiring biography or memoir
  ☐ Children's books
  ☐ Comics
- Writing down your negative thoughts and sealing them in an airtight container
- Identifying what you are feeling (Alcoholics Anonymous wisely recommends that people learn to recognize the HALT signals: hungry, angry, lonely, and tired)
- Making a phone call
- Tearing up paper (old phone books, newspaper, and so on)
- Turning every "should have," "must," "need to," and "wish I had" statement into a life-affirming thought (for instance, instead of saying, "I need to stop this," try saying, "I want to be free of this." From there you can move to, "I can be free of this." Perhaps you can even start to say, "With God's help, I *will* be free of this.")
- Watching a funny or uplifting movie
- Listening to a comedy tape
- Asking for help
- Contacting a help or support line

APPENDIX D

A Discussion Guide

I'd like to give you some suggested questions for discussion and reflection. I'm going to break this short conversation guide into two sections, including things you can discuss:

- With the self-injurer in your life
- With a trusted friend

THINGS TO DISCUSS WITH THE SELF-INJURER IN YOUR LIFE

Note: Use discernment with regard to timing and appropriateness for using these suggestions. The self-injurer in your life may not be ready right now to discuss his or her behavior with you. Perhaps you can start with one question or statement and see how the person you love responds. If he or she seems eager to talk, you can proceed at your own pace. If he or she appears reticent or downright resistant, it's best not to force discussion at this time.

1. Is there a certain time of day or situation that makes you feel like hurting yourself? Are there people in your life who seem to spark a desire to cut/burn/etc.?

2. Is there anything you're discussing with your therapist that you'd like to share with me?

3. Have I done or said anything that has been particularly helpful? Harmful?

4. Is there anything you've learned about self-injury that you'd like to share with me?

5. How can I pray for you?

THINGS TO DISCUSS WITH A TRUSTED FRIEND

Note: As far as talking with people who might need to know about the behavior of the person you love, here's what Wendy Lader and Karen Conterio suggest: "[_____ (name of the self-injurer you know)] is dealing with some serious emotional problems, and one of the ways she [or he] is coping is by harming herself [or himself]." They also recommend you "have some references and literature available for family members so they can quickly learn [he or she] is not a crazy person, that [he or she] is not necessarily in lethal danger, and that [he or she] is unlikely to harm anyone else."[1]

The following questions are not about informing others. They are intended to help you become the helper/understanding partner in recovery that the self-harmer in your life needs. The intensity and vulnerability may intimidate you at first. But being willing to explore these things can challenge you to become a genuine help to the self-wounder you know on his or her journey of healing.

1. Have you noticed anything about _____ (name of the self-injurer you know) that you think might be helpful for me to know?

2. Are there ways you've learned to deal with difficult situations in your own life or in the lives of people you love that might help me understand and come alongside _____ (name of the self-injurer you know)?

3. Have you noticed ways I communicate that might be shaming or that might prevent _____ (name of the self-injurer you know) from expressing his (or her) feelings?

4. Is there anything you see in me that might inadvertently spark _____ (name of the self-injurer you know) to hurt himself (or herself)?

5. Would you be willing to pray with me regularly?

NOTES

Chapter One: Then and Now

1. Howard Chua-Eoan et al., "Death of a Princess," *Time*, September 8, 1997, http://www.time.com/time/magazine/ article/0,9171,986949-1,00.html.
2. Charles, the ninth Earl Spencer, "Eulogy for Diana Frances Spencer, Princess of Wales," September 7, 1997, http://www .eulogybook.net/eulogy_princess_diana.html.
3. Marilee Strong, *A Bright Red Scream: Self-Mutilation and the Language of Pain* (New York: Penguin Books, 1998), 25.
4. Steven Levenkron, *Cutting: Understanding and Overcoming Self- Mutilation*, rev. ed. (New York: Norton, 1999), 10.
5. E. M. Pattison and J. Kahan, "The Deliberate Self-Harm Syndrome," *American Journal of Psychiatry* 140 (1983): 867–872.
6. V. J. Turner, *Secret Scars: Uncovering and Understanding the Addiction of Self-Injury* (Center City, MN: Hazelden Foundation, 2002).
7. Armando R. Favazza, *Bodies Under Siege: Self-mutilation and Body Modification in Culture and Psychiatry*, 2nd ed. (Baltimore, MD: The Johns Hopkins University Press, 1996), 225–261.
8. Karen Conterio, Wendy Lader, PhD, and Jennifer Kingson Bloom, *Bodily Harm: The Breakthrough Healing Program for Self- Injurers* (New York: Hyperion Press, 1998), first reference on page x.
9. Camelot Foundation, "Young People and Self Harm: A National

Inquiry: What Do We Already Know? Prevalence, Risk Factors, and Models of Intervention," 2004, http://www.selfharmuk.org/what.asp. Cited by Cornell University Family Life Development Center, "Cornell Research Program on Self-Injurious Behavior in Adolescents and Young Adults," http://www.crpsib.com/whatissi.asp?.

10. FACTIVA online database, Dow Jones Reuters Business Interactive LLC, accessed July 17, 2004. Cited by Cornell University Family Life Development Center, "Cornell Research Program on Self-Injurious Behavior in Adolescents and Young Adults," http://www.crpsib.com/whatissi.asp?.

11. Jennifer Radcliffe, "Self-Destructive 'Cutters' Living Their Lives on the Edge," *Los Angeles Daily News*, March 29, 2004, accessible for a fee through the archives at http://www.dailynews.com/Stories/0,1413,200~20954-2048086,00.html.

12. National Institute of Mental Health, "Women Hold Up Half the Sky: Women and Mental Health Research," 2001, http://www.nimh.nih.gov/publicat/womensoms.cfm.

13. Jeffrey Kluger, "The Cruelest Cut: Often It's the One Teens Inflict on Themselves. Why Are So Many American Kids Secretly Self-Mutilating?" *Time*, May 16, 2005, http://www.time.com/time/archive/preview/0,10987,1059046,00.html.

14. Kluger.

15. For help in synthesizing some of the historical information in the following section, I am indebted to the work done by Alexander V. Timofeyev, Katie Sharff, Nora Burns, and Rachel Outterson. You can access their study, copyrighted in 2002, at http://wso.williams.edu/~atimofey/self_mutilation/History/index.html.

16. Turner, 112.

17. C. S. Lewis, *The Lion, the Witch and the Wardrobe* (New York: HarperCollins, 1997), 132.

18. Lewis, 144.

19. Lewis, 150–151.

20. Levenkron, 10.

21. Thanks to Steven Levenkron for this excellent example.

Chapter Two: What Words Cannot Explain

1. Tracy Alderman, PhD, *The Scarred Soul: Understanding and Ending Self-Inflicted Violence* (Oakland, CA: New Harbinger Publications, Inc., 1997), 13.

2. Caroline Kettlewell, *Skin Game: A Memoir* (New York: St. Martin's Press, 1999), 13.

3. Patricia McCormick, *Cut* (New York: PUSH, a division of Scholastic, Inc., 2000), 122.

4. Rachel Houston, "Playing with Knives," *WORLD*, March 11, 2006, 32.

5. Philip's story can be found in Alderman, 65.

6. Alderman, 19.

7. Karen Conterio, Wendy Lader, PhD, and Jennifer Kingson Bloom, *Bodily Harm: The Breakthrough Healing Program for Self-Injurers* (New York: Hyperion Press, 1998), 130.

8. A. Favazza and K. Conterio, "Female Habitual Self-Mutilators," *Acta Psychiatrica Scandinavica* 79 (1989): 283–289.

9. Steven Levenkron, *Cutting: Understanding and Overcoming Self-Mutilation*, rev. ed. (New York: Norton, 1999), 38–39.

10. Jeffrey Kluger, "The Cruelest Cut: Often It's the One Teens Inflict on Themselves. Why Are So Many American Kids Secretly Self-Mutilating?" *Time*, May 16, 2005, http://www.time.com/time/archive/preview/0,10987,1059046,00.html.

11. Levenkron, 19.

12. Marilee Strong, *A Bright Red Scream: Self-Mutilation and the Language of Pain* (New York: Penguin Books, 1998), 9.

13. Strong, 44.

14. Strong, 44.

15. Kettlewell, 27.

16. Joan Jacobs Brumberg, *The Body Project: An Intimate History of*

American Girls (New York: Vintage Books, 1998), 169.

17. William Shakespeare, *Richard II*, ed. Roma Gill (Oxford: Oxford University Press, 2003), 4.1.294–297. References are to act, scene, and line.

18. Jan Sutton, *Healing the Hurt Within: Understand and Relieve the Suffering Behind Self-Destructive Behaviour* (Oxford: Pathways, 1999), 20.

19. Kettlewell, 111.

20. Alderman, 41.

21. Conterio, Lader, and Bloom, xi.

22. Jason Block, "Cutting and Self Mutilation," Psyke.org, http://www.psyke.org/faqs/cutting/.

23. Levenkron, 73–76.

24. Kettlewell, 60.

Chapter Three: Misery Loves Company

1. Many of the thoughts in this section have been adapted from Jerusha Clark, *Every Thought Captive: Battling the Toxic Beliefs That Separate Us from the Life We Crave* (Colorado Springs, CO: NavPress, 2005), 179–201.

2. Alina Salganicoff, PhD, Usha R. Ranji, MS, and Roberta Wyn, PhD, "Women and Health Care: A National Profile," Kaiser Family Foundation, July 2005, http://www.kff.org/womenshealth/upload/Women-and-Health-Care-A-National -Profile-Key-Findings-from-the-Kaiser-Women-s-Health-Survey .pdf.

3. National Institute of Mental Health, "Depression in Men," http://menanddepression.nimh.nih.gov/infopage.asp?ID=1.

4. Jesse Dillinger, "Depression: The Basics," audiotape one of two lectures titled *Depression and the Christian* (San Diego: Jesse Dillinger Enterprises, 2004).

5. *Webster's New Collegiate Dictionary* (Springfield, MA: G. & G. Merriam Webster Company, 1981), s.v. "Depression."

6. Dr. Dan B. Allender and Dr. Tremper Longman III, *The Cry of the Soul: How Our Emotions Reveal Our Deepest Questions About God* (Colorado Springs, CO: NavPress, 1994), 144.

7. Thank you to Caroline Kettlewell for using a wonderful image that gave me a foundation from which to integrate and develop my own thoughts.

8. B. Parry-Jones and W. L. Parry-Jones, "Self-Mutilation in Four Historical Cases of Bulimia," *British Journal of Psychiatry* 163 (1993): 394–401.

9. Marilee Strong, *A Bright Red Scream: Self-Mutilation and the Language of Pain* (New York: Penguin Books, 1998), 85.

10. Karen Conterio and Wendy Lader, PhD, "Self-Injury," *National Mental Health Association*, http://www.nmha.org/infoctr/ factsheets/selfinjury.cfm.

11. Dr. Armando Favazza, introduction to *A Bright Red Scream*, by Marilee Strong.

12. Strong, 79.

13. Strong, 84.

14. Dr. Dan B. Allender, *The Wounded Heart: Hope for Adult Victims of Childhood Sexual Abuse*, rev. ed. (Colorado Springs, CO: NavPress, 1995), 43.

15. Daniel G. Amen, MD, *Healing the Hardware of the Soul: How Making the Brain-Soul Connection Can Optimize Your Life, Love, and Spiritual Growth* (New York: Free Press, 2000), 45, 54.

16. Alice Miller, *Thou Shalt Not Be Aware: Society's Betrayal of the Child* (New York: Farrar, Straus, and Giroux, 1998), 315.

17. Strong, 38.

18. Steven Levenkron, *The Luckiest Girl in the World: A Young Skater Battles Her Self-Destructive Impulses* (New York: Penguin Books, 1997), 140.

19. Deb Martinson, "Self Injury Fact Sheet," *Multiplicity, Abuse & Healing Network*, 1999, http://www.m-a-h.net/library/selfinjury/ article-si-facts.htm.

20. Tracy Alderman, PhD, *The Scarred Soul: Understanding and Ending Self-Inflicted Violence* (Oakland, CA: New Harbinger Publications, Inc., 1997), 102–103.

21. Sharon Van Sell et al., "Help Stop Self-Injury," *Registered Nurse*, November 2005, 57. Also accessible at www.rnweb.com.

Chapter Four: Is It All in Their Head?

1. Marilee Strong, *A Bright Red Scream: Self-Mutilation and the Language of Pain* (New York: Penguin Books, 1998), 88.

2. Dharma Singh Khalsa, MD, and Cameron Stauth, "A Journey Down the Pain Pathway," in *The Pain Cure: The Proven Medical Program That Helps End Your Chronic Pain* (New York: Warner Books, 1999). Excerpt accessible at http://www. enotalone.com/ article/3356.html.

3. Daniel Kane, "How Your Brain Handles Love and Pain: Scanners Reveal Mechanisms Behind Empathy and Placebo Effect," *MSNBC*, updated February 19, 2004, http://msnbc.msn .com/id/4313263/.

4. J. Coid, B. Allolio, and L. H. Rees, "Raised Plasma Metenkephalin in Patients Who Habitually Mutilate Themselves," *Lancet* 1 (September 3, 1983): 545–546.

5. Philip David Zelazo, PhD, "The Development of Executive Function Across the Lifespan," *AboutKidsHealth*, June 24, 2005, http://www.aboutkidshealth.ca/ofhc/PrintNewsArticle .asp?articleID=4292.

6. Zelazo.

7. As told to Marilee Strong and reported in *A Bright Red Scream: Self-Mutilation and the Language of Pain*, 109–112.

8. Daniel G. Amen, MD, *Change Your Brain, Change Your Life: The Breakthrough Program for Conquering Anxiety, Depression, Obsessiveness, Anger, and Impulsiveness* (New York: Three Rivers Press, 1999), 53–54, 95–96, 132–133, 169–170, 202.

9. "Emerging Research Fronts: Comments," *Essential Science*

Indicators: Special Topics, August 2005, http://www.esi-topics
.com/erf/2005/august05-LarryCahill.html, emphasis added.

10. Strong, 92.

11. Lisa R. Ferentz, "Understanding Self-Injurious Behavior,"
Performance Resource Press, Summer 2002, http://www.prponline
.net/School/SAJ/Articles/understanding_self_injurious
_behavior.htm. Reprinted with permission from New York
University Child Study Center's electronic newsletter www
.aboutourkids.org, November/December 2001.

Chapter Five: How Will You Know?

1. Michelle Malkin, "The New Youth Craze: Self Mutilation,"
WorldNetDaily, February 23, 2005, http://www.worldnetdaily
.com/news/article.asp?ARTICLE_ID=42996.

2. By Goth, I mean teenagers who dress primarily in black, may
use makeup to decorate their skin or make it paler, paint their
lips and nails black, and so on. Most students who adopt this
style do not know that the Goth expression came out of the
San Francisco–based role-playing community, in which people
dressed and acted like vampires.

3. The descriptor Emo, which only recently came on the scene
and is therefore still "under construction," first identified young
people who listen to particular kinds of depressive, suicidal,
or violent music. But Emo goes beyond music preference. A
young woman in our youth group described Emo kids as ones
who "dress all in black, but aren't Gothic. They wear really
tight-fitting pants (some of the guys wear girls' pants) and shirts
that say things like, 'I hate my life.' Their hair is usually draped
across their face, almost to hide themselves. But you can see their
scars. . . . They don't hide those."

4. Steven Levenkron, *The Luckiest Girl in the World: A Young Skater
Battles Her Self-Destructive Impulses* (New York: Penguin Books,
1997), 77.

5. Patricia McCormick, *Cut* (New York: PUSH, a division of Scholastic, Inc., 2000), 119.
6. Melody Carlson, *Blade Silver: Color Me Scarred* (Colorado Springs, CO: TH1NK, 2005), 5.
7. Carlson, 90.
8. Caroline Kettlewell, *Skin Game: A Memoir* (New York: St. Martin's Press, 1999), 130–131.
9. Karen Conterio, Wendy Lader, PhD, and Jennifer Kingson Bloom, *Bodily Harm: The Breakthrough Healing Program for Self-Injurers* (New York: Hyperion, 1998), 97.
10. Sara Shandler, *Ophelia Speaks: Adolescent Girls Write About Their Search for Self* (New York: Harper Perennial, 1999), 44.
11. McCormick, 83.

Chapter Six: What Can I Do?

1. Deb Martinson, "Self Injury Fact Sheet," *Multiplicity, Abuse & Healing Network*, 1999, http://www.m-a-h.net/library/selfinjury/article-si-facts.htm, emphasis added.
2. Tracy Alderman, PhD, *The Scarred Soul: Understanding and Ending Self-Inflicted Violence* (Oakland, CA: New Harbinger Publications, Inc., 1997), 133.
3. Caroline Kettlewell, *Skin Game: A Memoir* (New York: St. Martin's Press, 1999), 20–21.

Chapter Seven: Dressing the Wounds

1. C. J. Sanderson, "Dialectical Behavior Therapy Frequently Asked Questions," *Behavioral Tech, LLC*, 2003, http://www.behavioraltech.com/downloads/dbtFaq_Cons.pdf.
2. Regents of the University of Michigan, "About Dialectical Behavior Therapy," *University of Michigan Department of Psychiatry*, last updated March 16, 2006, http://www.med.umich.edu/psych/amb/pated/dbted.htm.
3. Elliot Miller, "Theophostic Prayer Ministry: Christian Prayer,

Occult Visualization, or Secular Psychotherapy?" *Christian Research Journal*, 2006, http://www.equip.org/free/JAT206-1.htm.

4. New Creation Publishing, Inc., "What Is Theophostic Ministry?" *Theophostic Prayer Ministries*, 2006, http://www.theophostic.com/displaycommon.cfm?an=3.

5. Miller.

6. Miller.

7. EMDR International Association, "EMDRIA's Definition of Eye Movement Desensitization and Reprocessing (EMDR)," http://www.emdria.org/displaycommon.cfm?an=1&subarticlenbr=3.

8. EMDR International Association, "What Is the Actual EMDR Session Like?" http://www.emdria.org/displaycommon.cfm?an=1&subarticlenbr=5.

9. Dr. Ira Dressner, "Frequently Asked Questions," http://www.drdressner.com/questions.htm.

10. EMDR International Association, "How Does EMDR Work?" http://www.emdria.org/displaycommon.cfm?an=1&subarticlenbr=2.

11. EMDR International Association, "What Is EMDR?" http://www.emdria.org/displaycommon.cfm?an=1&subarticlenbr=56.

12. Bette Runck, "What Is Biofeedback?" *Division of Communication and Education, National Institute of Mental Health*, reprinted online by the Arizona Behavioral Health Associates, P.C., http://www.psychotherapy.com/bio.html.

13. Runck.

14. Steven Levenkron, *The Luckiest Girl in the World: A Young Skater Battles Her Self-Destructive Impulses* (New York: Penguin Books, 1997), 124.

Chapter Eight: When the Body Is Ravaged, the Soul Cries Out

1. All the quotations in the following section have been excerpted from "Only Once: A Testimony About Self Harm and Cutting,"

SloppyNoodle.com, http://www.sloppynoodle.com/selfharm
.shtml.

2. Chuck Swindoll, quoted in Earl R. Henslin, PhD, *Forgiven and Free: Learn How Bible Heroes with Feet of Clay Are Models for Your Recovery* (Nashville: Nelson, 1991), 119.

3. Lewis B. Smedes, *Shame and Grace: Healing the Shame We Don't Deserve* (San Francisco: HarperSanFrancisco, 1993), iii.

4. Smedes, 5.

5. John Bradshaw, *Bradshaw On: The Family: A New Way of Creating Solid Self-Esteem*, rev. ed. (Deerfield Beach, FL: Health Communications, Inc. 1990), 167.

6. Dr. Dan B. Allender and Dr. Tremper Longman III, *The Cry of the Soul: How Our Emotions Reveal Our Deepest Questions About God* (Colorado Springs, CO: NavPress, 1994), 164, 166.

7. Carl D. Schneider, PhD, *Shame, Exposure, and Privacy*, 2nd ed. (Boston: Beacon Press, 1977), chapters 3 and 4 excerpted at http://mediationmatters.com/Resources/res-shame.htm.

8. Smedes, 109.

9. Smedes, 107, 108.

10. Dr. Dan B. Allender, *The Wounded Heart: Hope for Adult Victims of Childhood Sexual Abuse*, rev. ed. (Colorado Springs, CO: NavPress, 1995), 209–210.

11. Dallas Willard, quoted in John Ortberg, "The 'Shyness' of God," *Christianity Today*, February 5, 2001, 67.

12. I am indebted to the work of the Lysamena Project on Self-Injury, http://www.self-injury.org/, which helped me identify how specific Scripture applies to self-harm.

13. Allender and Longman III, 150.

14. Also known as Communion, the Lord's Supper, and the Lord's Table.

15. James Frey, *A Million Little Pieces*, 2nd ed. (New York: Anchor Books, 2004), 266.

16. Sara Shandler, *Ophelia Speaks: Adolescent Girls Write About Their Search for Self* (New York: Harper Perennial, 1999), 21.

17. Leslie F. Brandt, *Psalms Now* (St. Louis, MO: Concordia, 1973), 162.

18. Allender, 233.

19. Allender, 233.

20. Hannah Arendt, *The Human Condition* (Chicago: University of Chicago Press, 1958), 212–213.

21. Many of the thoughts in this section are taken from Jerusha Clark, *Every Thought Captive: Battling the Toxic Beliefs That Separate Us from the Life We Crave* (Colorado Springs, CO: TH1NK, 2006), 94.

A Benediction

1. Leslie F. Brandt, *Psalms Now* (St. Louis, MO: Concordia, 1973), 142–143.

Appendix C: Alternatives to Self-Injurious Behavior

1. For portions of this section, I am grateful for the work done by Kay to amass a list of alternatives to self-inflicted violence. See www.selfinjury.net. Follow the What is. . . ? link and then click on Alternatives to SI.

Appendix D: A Discussion Guide

1. Karen Conterio, Wendy Lader, PhD, and Jennifer Kingson Bloom, *Bodily Harm: The Breakthrough Healing Program for Self-Injurers* (New York: Hyperion, 1998), 165–166.

ABOUT THE AUTHORS

JERUSHA CLARK is the coauthor of several best-selling books, including *I Gave Dating a Chance*. While researching for her recently released book *Every Thought Captive*, she recognized the need for a book confronting the important issue of self-injury. A graduate of Rice University, Jerusha works with teenagers alongside her husband, a high school pastor in Southern California. She also thoroughly enjoys being a mommy to daughters Jocelyn and Jasmine.

DR. EARL HENSLIN has a doctorate in clinical psychology and is licensed in California as a Marriage and Family Therapist. He has authored four books, *You Are Your Father's Daughter*, *Man to Man*, *Forgiven and Free*, and *Off the Cliff*, and is the coauthor of *Secrets of Your Family Tree*. Dr. Henslin has a clinic in Southern California and has spoken nationally and internationally on relationships, addictions, and the neurobiology of relationships.

MORE THINK BOOKS FOR FINDING HOPE, HELP, AND HEALING.

Every Thought Captive

Jerusha Clark   1-57683-868-4

Drawing from personal experiences, including struggles with anorexia and depression, best-selling author Jerusha Clark shares the freedom found in shifting our thoughts from the everyday to the eternal.

Blade Silver: Color Me Scarred

Melody Carlson   1-57683-535-9

In this fictional story, Ruth Wallace uses cutting as a way to deal with the trauma of a dysfunctional family. As she attempts to stop cutting, her family life deteriorates further to the point that Ruth isn't sure she'll ever be able to stop. She needs help, but can she find it before this habit threatens her life?

THINK ®   NAVPRESS ®
BRINGING TRUTH TO LIFE
www.navpress.com

To order copies, visit your local Christian bookstore,
call NavPress at 1-800-366-7788, or log on to www.navpress.com.
To locate a Christian bookstore near you,
call 1-800-991-7747.